Losing Your Job
& Finding Yourself

Losing Your Job & Finding Yourself

Memoir, Myths, and Methods for Inventive Career Transitions

Nancy Brout, M.S.Ed.

Words**P**erfected LLC

Disclaimer

Every reasonable effort has been made to ensure the information (including internet addresses) in this book is correct and current as of the time of publication. Readers are encouraged to use common sense and discretion while using any information in this book, which will best serve as a general source of information and ideas. No amount of information can guarantee success in overcoming job loss, attaining a job, or changing careers.

The author and the publisher assume no responsibility for errors, omissions, or inaccuracies. Further, the author and publisher have no control over and do not assume any responsibility for third-party websites or their content.

The contents of this book are for educational purposes only and should not be viewed as professional advice of any kind. Where legal, financial, psychological, medical, or other advice is required, you should always consult a qualified professional to obtain advice that pertains to your specific situation and needs.

Cover Sculpture: *Freedom*, Zenos Frudakis
Photographs: Joseph Painter
Cover Design: Bonnie Brout and Elisha Iozzi

For Bryan—my heart
Erna, David, Bonnie, and Jaylan—my family

... and everyone who ever lost a job they wanted to keep—
perhaps more than once

*Choose a job you love, and you will never
have to work a day in your life.*
— Confucius

Foreword

It might seem like an impossible dream to find work you love, especially if you lost a job you wanted to keep. *Losing Your Job & Finding Yourself* is a rare gift for professionals who want to figure out what's next in their careers.

When job loss and turbulence come with feeling like there's nowhere to go, Nancy's honest and insightful memoir is a beacon for possibility, and a roadmap for how to get to that job that means so much.

Nancy's story begins with one of those experiences that shifts your whole world. At age 53, just shy of 20 years with a company, she was let go. Her personal insights and transformation did not come easily. The emotional and literal journey to starting the job she always wanted was volatile, difficult, joyous, and filled with amazing people.

We are the beneficiaries as Nancy shares practical methods for job search and networking that will enable you to approach your transition as a personal journey toward a fulfilling next role, not just a job. She offers inspiration, courage, and a can-do spirit—exactly what you might need to sustain your focus on the way to your goal.

Her key lesson? You must do the work. Immersing yourself in her memoir and innovative approaches will inspire you to make things happen for yourself. You can do this—and reading Nancy's story will help you get to the best job you ever had—any time you need to. This timeless guide will see you through career challenges and transitions for the rest of your life.

DR. PAULETTE GABRIEL
PRESIDENT, KEY LEADERSHIP

TABLE OF CONTENTS

Self-Assessments | Accomplishment Stories: (PARS) |
Online Job Searches and Daily Alerts | Departure
Statement | Elevator Pitch | Professional Brand | Business
Cards | LinkedIn Profile and Connections | Résumé(s) |
Cover Letters | Online Applications and Applicant
Tracking Systems (ATS) | One-Page Networking Profile
With Target Companies | Networking With Purpose:
Quality vs. Quantity of Connections | Network Tracking
Report | Using LinkedIn to Get Introduced | Recruiters |
Reasons to Volunteer | Alternative Work Arrangements:
Contract/Temporary, Part-Time, Freelance | Updating
Your Skills: New Certifications and/or Courses | Personal
or Professional Website | Social Media and Blogging |

PART I

THE BACKSTORY: WRITTEN FOR ME AND YOU

The purpose of life is to discover your gift;
the work of life is to develop it;
and the meaning of life is to
give your gift away.
– UNKNOWN SOURCE

20 Great Years Minus 7 Days: Losing a Job I Thought I Wanted to Keep

My job was eliminated just shy of 20 years at one company. As they say in the U.K., I had become redundant. At 53 years old, I was escorted out of the building.

Twelve turbulent months later, I began a new, purpose-driven chapter in my life and work. This is a personal and universal story of the despair, recovery, discovery, and triumph many of us face when our careers fall apart or we want to make a change. Then, at the end of a quest, we find work we are meant to do.

The reality or possibility of losing our jobs has permeated our lives since the Global financial crisis hit in December 2007. Aspects of my experience are shared by many who ever lost a job they wanted to keep (or thought they did).

If it's happened to you or someone close, you know losing a job can feel devastating and set off an emotional roller coaster. The experience can be fraught with many dark moments of hurt, anger, anxiety, and depression. But, over time, as you heal and gain perspective, it can bring opportunities you never imagined—and might not have discovered any other way.

My midlife career transition was one of the most difficult experiences of my life. It was also a gift of time to explore, find myself, and discover work I loved. After finally figuring out what I did and did not want to do, I invented the next chapter of my life and career, and landed in an extraordinary job.

As time passed beyond that dreadful day of termination, I gained new perspectives and became grateful about no longer being at the company that eliminated my job. This new ground was not gained easily. But, along the way, I came to believe everything happened for a reason. When one door closed, others opened, leading to fulfilling work that made me happy.

Writing and editing has been a central and satisfying element of my career spanning more than 30 years. I often thought about writing a book someday. But I never had a subject that got my creative juices flowing—until I lost my job. Seventeen days later, unable to sleep past 5:00 a.m., I started a journal. Menopause had already wreaked havoc on my ability to sleep through the night. Being unemployed made a good night's sleep more impossible.

My journal evolved into a golden opportunity to write that elusive book in the sky. What started as a vehicle for emotional catharsis and self-discovery became an intellectual challenge and opportunity to help others create their own next chapters.

New Realities:
Losing Our Jobs and Finding Ourselves

With job security long gone, millions of us get lost at sea during our careers—at least once. Your transitions and triumphs will differ from mine and could take many directions. Your next move could be any combination of full-time, part-time, freelance, or not working at all. You might join over 50 million Americans who are freelancing—mostly by choice.

However your situation plays out, I aimed to shed light on what we experience during challenging career changes. If you relate to any of these situations, my story is likely to resonate for you:

1. In transition after losing a job you wanted to keep, especially at age 50+/-

2. Staying too long in a job you would rather lose

3. Being a Hard-to-Define Professional with many transferable skills that are not easily categorized into a single, clearly defined vocation

4. Considering a career change

5. Trying to figure out what you *can* and *want* to do at any stage of your career (including recent graduates and younger employees who haven't developed clear professional identities)

6. Wishing you could do purpose-driven work you care about deeply

All of these scenarios are Inventive Career Transitions. They require activities that differ from a standard job search for a clearly defined role. While experiencing all six circumstances above, I shifted directions multiple times, and developed job search methods that generated interviews and offers. These methods differ from what most career coaches advise.

Through my own and others' transitions, I developed a clear point of view about search and networking activities that are more and less effective. My perspectives evolved into a compelling purpose to share what I learned to help others discover what they *can* and *want* to do, and then make it happen.

If you want to just find a new job—and any job will do—this book might not be for you. If you are embarking on a transition through which you want to find yourself, reinvent your career, and love your work—keep reading. And remember, *all* thoughts, feelings, actions, and results you encounter along the way are steps toward your next destination.

Dispelling Myths:
The Hidden Job Market and Networking

Conventional wisdom is that networking is *the best*, if not *the only* way to land a new job. People in transition are often told, "It's *all* about networking and being in the right place at the right time." You've probably heard 80% of jobs are *never* advertised.

Given this so-called "hidden job market," job seekers are told to spend 80% to 90% of their time networking, ideally face-to-face, with everyone they can. Common advice is to spend no more than 10% to 20% of your job search time online or chasing recruiters. The widely held belief that 80% of jobs are *never* advertised can be traced back to the 1970s and 1980s. Repeated so often, many view it as reality.

Even more extreme, you may have been told to *never* apply for jobs posted online, and to pursue them *only* through networking. A statistic cited at a 2016 recruiting conference claimed that applying through job boards resulted in hiring only 0.1% of the time. A 2016 blog post stated that résumés are dying.

So, let's dispel these myths:

- Going back to 1982, I landed *all* my jobs by applying for advertised jobs—not through networking. The "hidden job market" never matched my experience.

- Many people I know have applied for and landed advertised positions, with and without networking assistance.

- Hiring practices evolved dramatically since the advent of the internet, and new methods emerge every day.

- While résumés *are* getting more creative, it will be many years before they are no longer a standard item in every job search toolkit.

If it were ever true, the 80% hidden-job-market statistic should have become extinct decades ago. Sure, networking to gain introductions and internal referrals is a great way to get hired. But, as essential as networking is, viewing it as the *only* way to get hired blatantly rejects the potency of effective online job search activities.

The power of online methods for job search and networking is drastically underestimated and growing exponentially.

Job seekers who don't use online channels to generate interviews and offers are missing primary pathways to land their next jobs.

The rapidly changing tide in how employees are being hired is gaining recognition. One example is a LinkedIn infographic, "Global Trends That Will Shape Recruiting In 2015" (https://business.linkedin.com/talent-solutions/blog/2014/11/the-global-trends-that-will-shape-recruiting-in-2015). In 2011, the top source for *new hires* was employee referrals. In 2014, top sources were internet job boards (e.g., Indeed: 42%, up 15% since 2011) and social professional networks (e.g., LinkedIn: 38%, up 73% since 2011).

In a report from SilkRoad, "Top Sources of Hire 2015" (http://hr1.silkroad.com/sm-top-sources-of-hire), 39% of *hires* were made through online job search engines, job boards, and career sites. A related article worth reading is "The Vanishing Hidden Job Market" (http://www.resumehacking.com/hidden-job-market-vanishing).

These trends are consistent with my recent search and the experiences of job seekers I have coached. Almost all of my interviews and offers resulted from applying online for advertised positions. This included being offered a position that had more than 450 applicants—without connections or introductions in the organization.

An essential caveat is that the pace of change in recruiting and job search practices is accelerating as quickly as the internet, social media, and mobile technology. As favored online recruiting channels come and go faster than any book can keep up with, job seekers must stay current to leverage those that work best for their searches.

New Solutions:
The Winning Job Search Formula is
Online AND Networking

Moving from myths to more realities, it *is* possible to land great jobs by applying online. And more people are doing so every day. My own and countless others' results contradict almost everything career management professionals have told you. Online applications, with superior quality résumés and cover letters, do *not* always get lost in the black hole. Many *do* get through automated systems and *are* seen by human eyes. Think about it. Why would hundreds of thousands of robust job descriptions be posted online if nobody intended to hire this way?

Skeptics might argue that companies post jobs because the Federal Equal Employment Opportunity Commission (EEOC) requires them to. Guess what? This is another myth. A well-known EEOC law prohibits discrimination in hiring based on race, color, religion, sex (including gender identity, sexual orientation, and pregnancy), national origin, age (40 or older), disability, or genetic information. To comply with this law, some employers (e.g., government and government contractors) advertise and use applicant tracking systems to capture statistics for all job openings. But these are employer policies, not legal requirements.

I'm not saying online job search methods are right and networking is wrong. But emphasizing online resources is different, and significantly undervalued by many professionals. A multi-pronged approach wins the day, and is the basis for my Sweet Spot Job Search Method.

While emphasizing online methods, it *is* also vital to build and nurture a valuable professional network. When applying

7

for jobs, networking within that company *can* increase your chances of advancing through more rounds in the hiring process. But it is *not* the only way, nor is it always necessary.

It's also true that the likelihood of landing a job through networking rather than online applications rises with the level of the job. While many VP-level jobs are posted and filled through online channels, I've met people at and above this level who have never applied for advertised positions.

Even if you conduct your search through 100% networking and never apply online—if you consider yourself a Hard-to-Define Professional, or if you are considering a career change—you will find valuable information here. And, as specific recruiting and search methods change quickly, shared experiences of job loss and professional reinvention endure through time.

How This Book Differs From Career Management and Job Search Guides

This hybrid memoir and guide for Inventive Career Transitions diverges from most books in the career transition and job search genre.

My career evolved through four rare and fulfilling jobs. And, against the odds, I made three big directional shifts. As a Baby Boomer, I landed my previous jobs by responding to classified ads in the printed newspaper. If you were born after the late 1960s, you might have no idea what a printed job ad looks like. This was more than 20 years before the internet and LinkedIn existed.

This time, I conducted a 21st century, web-enabled job search and pursued four search strategies. Activities included applying online with high-quality documents, leveraging LinkedIn to increase my chances of getting noticed, and learning to enjoy targeted networking—what I call networking with purpose.

The vast ocean of online career management resources is overwhelming. Not drowning in it requires focus, selective navigation, and discipline. My intent is to provide an inspiring catalyst and efficient resource to help you navigate these career transition challenges:

1. **Emotional comfort, courage, and confidence during a stressful time:**
   - Understand common emotional reactions to unexpected job loss
   - Gain confidence and new ways to think about a difficult career transition
   - Appreciate opportunities to find greater fulfillment in your life and work

2. **Inspiration and methods to explore, discover, and articulate what you _can_ and _want_ to do next:**
   - Identify work-related needs, goals, and desires
   - Define transferable skills and a unique value proposition
   - Be inspired to find purpose-driven work you care about, with courage and confidence to shift gears and find work you love

3. **Activities to define and find sweet spot jobs to pursue:**
   - Learn methods and skills to find exciting new opportunities through online resources and networking with purpose

4. **Proven methods to generate interviews and offers, and land a job that makes you happy:**
   - Optimize your time and efforts by leveraging the experiences, activities, and tools that were most and least effective for me and people I have coached
   - Learn about recruiting and job search practices that require active monitoring to stay current

One of my greatest pleasures is coaching others through career transitions: clarifying personal and professional goals; exploring options; and connecting with resources, people, and organizations to achieve new aspirations.

This book is written in four parts. Beyond my story, it provides real-world guidance for people who don't have outplacement or career coaching support, and complements these services for those who do. Either way, I am honored by your decision to read it.

PART I: The Backstory introduces how my perspectives on career transitions differ from conventional wisdom. This section also explains how the book is structured, how you can benefit from reading it, and why I wrote it.

PART II: Long and Winding Road From Despair to Triumph is a memoir about my journey through losing my job, finding myself, and inventing my triumphant next chapter. Many people see themselves in my memoir, and it resonates deeply if you ever lost a job you wanted to keep.

My memoir is sprinkled with subsequent reflections, insights, and practical tips for any career transition. Because of this structure, the rhythm naturally undulates among past, present, and future tenses. Insights have a light bulb icon; Practical Tips have a check mark icon.

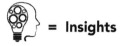 = Insights    = Practical Tips

PART III: The Art of Inventive Career Transitions includes perspectives on the multigenerational workforce, a retrospective of my unconventional career as a Hard-to-Define Professional, and opportunities to consider what this might mean for you.

At a high level, what differentiates mid-career Hard-to-Define Professionals is the diversity of roles and responsibilities we've had. We are not clearly defined as an actuarial, engineering, finance, HR, IT, marketing, operations, project management, sales, or any other type of professional. In contrast, we've had several less-distinct roles, contributing to typical functions in atypical ways. We've accomplished many things, added value and had a positive impact in many places, and developed a broad array of transferable skills we like to use in our work.

Everyone can benefit from other perspectives when navigating their careers. But being a "Swiss Army knife" with varied experiences that don't fit into a single vocation presents special challenges during transitions. Many of these challenges are shared by recent graduates and younger employees who have not developed clear professional identities.

For example, a standard element of any job search toolkit is an elevator pitch. This is a succinct description of your capabilities, what you want to do, and target companies where you would like to work. But you can't create this if you don't know, or can't articulate what you *can* and *want* to do next. Being in this situation makes it especially difficult to network productively for introductions and job leads.

PART IV: Sweet Spot Job Search Method provides an overall job search framework that includes online methods, superior marketing documents, and targeted networking. Expanding on the insights and tips throughout my memoir, 25 Activities are a compilation of practical search and networking methods to reference as you create your next chapter. They are organized in the order you are most likely to use them. Each features tips on the activities that were most and least effective during my recent transition.

As you work through the 25 Activities, please remember the earlier caveat about how quickly recruiting and job search practices are evolving. Some activities that worked for me might be obsolete when you read about them.

How Long Does it Take to Land a New Job?

A serious job search is more than a full-time job. Many job seekers underestimate how much patience and persistence is required to land a job that meets their needs and aspirations. Some get frustrated after a few weeks of submitting applications and networking. Reality check, please!

Finding a job that's a great fit can be like finding a needle in a haystack. This is especially true for Hard-to-Define Professionals and people who want to shift directions. Discovering and fulfilling your purpose or passion through work requires even more commitment and perseverance. This is where methods for Inventive Career Transitions become most important.

A traditional rule of thumb is to expect it to take one month for every $10,000 in base salary (e.g., 12 months for a $120,000 base salary). According to the executive-level website, The Ladders (https://www.theladders.com), searching for a $100,000 job takes five months plus one month for each significant factor you want to change (e.g., industry, function, location). It's reasonable to expect it to take longer as you aspire to higher-level roles that are inherently less prevalent. These guidelines are consistent with my experience.

If financial pressures require you to generate income sooner rather than later, you might need to find interim solutions, often called bridge jobs.

Regardless of how much time you have to find your next job, you will implement many of the 25 Activities described in PART IV. Doing this work with proactive diligence and discipline is no guarantee you will land more quickly. But you are much less likely to land a sweet spot or dream job in your target timeframe if you don't do the work.

Becoming an Author:
Meet Sententia, My Muse

Before you dive into my memoir, I reflected on becoming an author as this book took shape. According to a survey cited in *The New York Times* in 2002, 81% of Americans aspired to write a book. With the explosion of memoirs and self-publishing, I suspect that percentage has increased. But, if you are in the minority—never imagining a book marinates within—you might want to skip to my memoir in PART II. Aspiring author or not, you will learn more about me and my quirks if you keep reading this section.

I wrote this book because I had to. Most of these words poured out of me, and I had no choice but to put them on paper. As long as I can remember, writing has been my best method to clarify my point of view for myself and others. Like many writers, I often don't know what I think about something until I write about it.

For many years, composing copy on a computer keyboard has felt as though I am being inspired by my Muse, who is both a writer and a concert pianist. I don't play the piano, but words seem to travel through my fingers, onto the page, as if they are a musical score waiting to be played.

While writing this book, I named my Muse Sententia, Goddess of Words and Meaning. Sententia means *sentence* in Latin, as well as thought, meaning, and purpose. In plural form, sententiae can refer to a compilation of information for those about to enter a common experience—in this case, a career transition.

Sententia seemed to speak through me at my keyboard. She also sparked new ideas almost every time I stepped away from my computer. She often joined me in the shower, in my car, and during conversations with my husband when I was distracted by listening to her instead of him.

With Sententia on my shoulder, I did a lot of journal writing for three months after losing my job. She took a break in months four through eleven when my job search was in high gear, followed by a major setback. After this long absence, she returned in month twelve, inspiring me to write again as my next chapter took shape.

If you are interested in learning more about how artists and writers experience their Muse, *The War of Art* by Steven Pressfield is a great read. With his permission, several fascinating quotes about having a Muse are included at the end of this section.

As I wrote and edited this book, I gained a new understanding about why so many authors thank others for supporting them through their intensively obsessive writing periods. At times, I was so engrossed in writing and editing, I didn't hear what was going on around me. I didn't hear my husband talking to me. I missed the laundry completion signal I usually hear like a mother hears her baby cry. I almost started a fire when I didn't hear the timer and hard-boiled eggs exploded on the stove.

When I wasn't writing, many conversations ignited ideas and words I had to jot down so I could put them in their rightful places later. Once I had a new thought out of my head, captured on paper, I could move on or get back to sleep—but not before.

The first draft of this book was written within 18 months of losing my job. This was one of the most challenging periods of my life, and I worked longer hours on my search than I typically had in my jobs. I'm not sure how I found the time and stamina to write, but I couldn't walk away and *not* write. With strong conviction this book was meant to be, I was compelled to make it a reality.

Besides being driven by creative energy, persevering longer than three years to publish this was consistent with aspects of my personality that show up throughout my story. Some of the ways I handle stress match colloquial views of an Obsessive-Compulsive Disorder (OCD)—set off when I want to regain a sense of control over my circumstances. It made perfect sense that losing my job triggered a need to do things that made me feel I was in control.

Rather than an Achilles' heel, the positive aspects of my brand of OCD are being Organized, Committed, and Determined. Along with bringing strong organization to everything I do, I've always needed my surroundings to be organized precisely, with my belongings exactly where I want them. For example, my workspace must be set up *just right* for me to be comfortable and productive. My sister and I have laughed about me being like the princess in *The Princess and the Pea* who can't sleep because there's a pea under her mattress. Persnickety? Yep, that would be me.

Being organized, committed, and determined are valuable strengths when I set my mind to do something I think is important. When I care about something, like publishing this book, I can conquer many barriers to get it done.

These strengths also lead me to dive into activities with gusto, committing significant time, money, and brain space. Friends and family often admire my ability to accomplish whatever I set my mind to. But, knowing I take things on with intensity, I sometimes need time to rev up my motivation to start something new.

Both positive and negative, obsessive-compulsive behavior also shows up in my powerful perfectionistic streak. Being hypercritical makes it hard to stop working to improve most things I do. Endlessly editing my job search documents and this book are clear examples of this irresistible urge. My harsh inner critic is rarely satisfied that anything I do is perfect enough. When my husband feels criticized, I try to get him to imagine how it feels to be me.

As my reinvention progressed, writing provided a powerful emotional and creative outlet. Rather than dwelling on the negative aspects of my job elimination, it kept me energized and focused on something constructive. I needed to manage the time and energy I put into writing so it didn't divert too much attention from my career transition work.

While the words and pages kept flowing, I felt like I was meant to write this book. I didn't know how it would evolve, but it felt like an essential element of my transformation. On the second anniversary of losing my job, I shared the first draft manuscript with nine people who provided feedback. Besides ironic timing, this felt like a remarkable accomplishment. Upon the third anniversary, I was preparing to publish *Losing Your Job & Finding Yourself.*

The War of Art
Break Through the Blocks and
Win Your Inner Creative Battles
Steven Pressfield, Black Irish Entertainment LLC

These flashes of creative genius seem to arrive from out of the blue for the obvious reason: They come from the unconscious mind. In short, if the Muse exists, she does not whisper to the untalented (Foreword).

This is the other secret that real artists know and wannabe writers don't. When we sit down to do our work, power concentrates around us. The Muse takes note of our dedication. She approves. We have earned favor in her sight. When we sit down to work, we become like a magnetized rod that attracts iron filings. Ideas come. Insights accrete (pg. 108).

By Blake's model, as I understand it, it's as though the Fifth Symphony existed already in that higher sphere, before Beethoven sat down and played dah-dah-dah-DUM. The catch was this: The work existed only as potential—without a body, so to speak. It wasn't music yet. You couldn't play it. You couldn't hear it.

It needed someone. It needed a corporeal being, a human, an artist (or more precisely a *genius*, in the Latin sense of "soul" or "animating spirit") to bring it into being on this material plane. So the Muse whispered in Beethoven's ear.

Maybe she hummed a few bars into a million other ears. But no one else heard her. Only Beethoven got it. He brought it forth. He made the Fifth Symphony a "creation of time," which "eternity" could be "in love with" (pg. 117).

... your Muse is you, the best part of yourself, where your finest and only true work comes from (pg. 153).

PART II

MEMOIR: LONG AND WINDING ROAD FROM DESPAIR TO TRIUMPH

When you're going through hell,
keep going.
— WINSTON CHURCHILL

D-Day:
Is "D" for Despair or Destiny?

This was the day the layoffs would happen. But I was still in denial it would happen to me. As soon as I entered the lobby, I was met by my boss and escorted to Human Resources. *Oh shit, this is it.*

Like a scared and stubborn puppy, I felt like I was being dragged by my leash to a place I didn't want to go. I said something like, "You're letting me go, aren't you? Twenty f-bombing years and this is what happens? You've got to be kidding me!" Yep, I dropped the f-bomb.

Sinking heavily into a chair in the head of HR's office, it felt like I had rocks in my pockets. Totally unhinged, I couldn't focus on what my boss said about enjoying working with me and my valuable contributions to the company. Once my boss left the room, the head of HR gave me my gray folder of separation information and the form I had to sign to acknowledge receipt. We both knew my anger and distress would prevent me from absorbing what he said about the materials and what I needed to do. He was just doing his job, and my life just changed dramatically.

When we were done, he introduced me to my career coach from an outplacement firm. We shook hands before I said something like "I can't talk to you; you work for the company!" My coach explained the role of being a resource for me, and not discussing our conversations with anyone. Although never sure how true that was, I spent little time worrying about it. We finished our conversation and agreed I would get in touch when I was ready to talk. I sensed the relationship would be helpful, but I wasn't ready for help.

Onward to the finale. I turned down the offer to come back to the building on a different day to collect my belongings. It was almost a one-hour drive from home, and I didn't want to go back for many reasons.

With supervision, I packed a few boxes and was escorted through the hallways and out of the building. An out-of-body experience, I felt like a transparent ghost. Sounds were muffled as if I were walking in slow motion under water. I didn't make eye contact with anyone and felt intensely humiliated.

I drove to a neighboring corporate center parking lot and shattered into pieces. With sobbing tears, profound hurt, and seething anger, I called my husband and my mother to tell them I lost my job. My husband left work and met me at home.

In my irrational state of mind, I skimmed my separation documents but couldn't absorb any of the information. Of course, it made no sense that I even tried. More fitting for the situation, I cried and screamed, crawled into bed, and fell apart for the afternoon. I don't remember the rest of that dreadful day.

Over the years, I had spoken with former coworkers who lost their jobs under similar circumstances. Some handled the scenario quite differently. They said polite things and sent notes about how grateful they were for the opportunities and experiences they had at the company.

A few weeks later, when I gained distance and calmed down from my acute reactions, I thought back to my departure scene. I wished I had maybe said something about it having been 20 *great* years. But several close friends and family members supported what I did say—especially the f-bomb.

 Insights: There Has to Be a Better Way to Lay People Off—or Decide Not To

I joined the alumni association of former employees who stay in touch and support one another. Some of us were close colleagues, some of us never worked on projects together, and some of us had even had tension or conflicts with each other. Whatever had happened between us while working at the company, it no longer mattered.

You've probably experienced or witnessed common practices for orchestrating layoffs. People who lose their jobs this way describe the most demeaning parts of the experience—the unexpected ambush, being escorted out of the building, and having no opportunity to work through a transition with their successor(s). Common sentiments are feeling intensely insulted and humiliated by being treated like a criminal. My hurt and anger faded over time. But more than two years later, deeply embedded residue resurfaced with surprising intensity.

It's a curious phenomenon that people whose jobs are eliminated are typically prohibited from accessing their files. But those who voluntarily resign, giving a few weeks' or months' notice, usually have full access to their materials. Some industries (e.g., financial services) are less likely to allow this than others.

Sure, emotions are likely to differ based on whether someone leaves a company voluntarily or involuntarily. A person in the former situation is likely in control of their emotions, while the latter might be angry, volatile, or retaliatory. However, what's the difference between their intentions to have samples of their work and other materials they brought to the company?

After being escorted out of a building, many people engage in candid conversations about their former employer. Over time, this could damage a company's reputation and ability to attract and retain employees who feel any loyalty when other opportunities come their way.

Some companies have chosen different ways to treat people through a layoff process. Employees are sometimes told weeks or months in advance, and encouraged to stay (with or without extra compensation) to help implement the transition. Some companies create a separate workspace in which soon-to-be-separated employees begin their transition process.

Having time to calmly work through transferring responsibilities, technology, and other changes could smooth the experience for everyone. For adults who appreciate time to transfer work and begin their transition process, it could reduce the anguish and negative sentiments that often come with sudden dismissals.

Executives across the globe would benefit by engaging in thoughtful dialogue about the financial and human impact of downsizing. Topics to explore include:

- Assumptions behind the pervasive layoff mentality
- Extent to which layoffs achieve financial intentions
- Alternative ways to achieve financial results
- Fallout from executives receiving huge bonuses after cutting expenses through mass layoffs
- Impact of layoffs for those who leave and those who remain
- Creative ways to manage staff reductions and help people through job loss

New ways to think about whether and how to reduce staff could benefit companies, those who lose their jobs, those left behind, those who consider joining the company, and those just entering the workforce. Emerging perspectives and research on this topic can be found in "How Layoffs Hurt Companies" (http://knowledge.wharton.upenn.edu/article/how-layoffs-cost-companies).

Before D-Day: Denying Signs of Change

Over the course of 20 years, my work was interesting and challenging, and my responsibilities evolved in many satisfying directions. I enjoyed every opportunity to build and apply a wide range of transferable skills. Progressing through numerous promotions, I reached the level of assistant vice president. Aspects of my role were like chief of staff and special assistant to CEO roles in other organizations.

I was fortunate to report to the chairman and CEO for 16 years. Steering the business in a purpose- and values-driven manner, he was an admirable leader, a lifelong learner, and a great person to collaborate with. Throughout my tenure, I worked closely with the executive team and external consultants on company-wide initiatives that impacted strategic alignment, employee engagement, and customer loyalty.

During my last five years at the company, there was a gradual transition to a new CEO. As leadership changes evolved, so did my role and reporting relationship. In my last two-and-a-half years at the company, my boss retired and I was moved into the marketing and communications department, reporting to a different member of the executive team. As the succession progressed, I became less and less involved with the top leadership team.

I should have paid more attention to these gradual, yet tectonic shifts. While still enjoying my job and the people I worked with, I felt increasingly marginalized. It seemed like I had to work extra hard to demonstrate the value I was adding. I kept my head down and thought I wanted to stay at the company as long as possible, or until I was ready to leave on my own terms. Unfortunately, I didn't explore external opportunities or prepare myself for the job market during this leadership transition.

Summer in Denial

Many employees knew the company had to cut expenses— nothing out of the ordinary for businesses in any economic climate. Based on experience, it was a sure bet people would be laid off. The executives would choose a date to orchestrate the event.

As the summer progressed, I wondered if I would be on the layoff list this time. My husband and I discussed what I should do to prepare for the possibility I would not have a seat at the end of this round of musical chairs. But several assumptions led me to a naïve conclusion this would never happen to me. I convinced myself that my senior staff role made me indispensable and irreplaceable. I was betting on having contributed to the company's success, surviving prior layoffs, and being close to my 20th anniversary.

While previously supporting my husband through an extended period of unemployment, he often said he would be there to support me in a similar situation. Convinced I would leave the company when I was ready to make a change, I was operating under the mistaken belief this day would never come.

Looking back over the weeks leading up to the day the layoffs happened, I missed several clear signals I would, in fact, be walking out the door. For example:

- As part of a building renovation, my department was moving to a different wing. Everyone around me was packing their red plastic crates, but nobody gave me instructions to prepare for the move.

- Despite being scheduled to get a new laptop in September, information about the upgrade stopped coming my way.

- It was the month of my anniversary for 20 years of service, but I didn't receive my recognition packet to choose a gift.

Why didn't I pay more attention to these obvious clues? As the stage was being set, I was still involved in important projects, getting positive feedback about my work, and scheduled to attend meetings beyond the summer. And so, I thought, maybe I *would* still be employed after this layoff. A few days before D-Day, I happened to see a stack of gray folders. I wondered, but still fooled myself into believing my name wasn't on any of them.

In my unfortunate state of denial, I kept working as though nothing was about to change for me. I took no actions to prepare myself for the possibility it could be my turn. Clearly, my head was buried in the sand.

Month 1: Recovery
Setting Up My Home Office, Processing Emotions, Preparing for Next Steps

The best way out is always through.
— ROBERT FROST

Setting Up My Home Office
Rather than staying in bed and falling apart, my first order of business was getting set up to be productive at home. Being busy and relentlessly task-oriented prevented me from spiraling down the drain into painfully raw emotions.

Unfortunately, I had combined all business and personal use on a company-owned laptop, email address, and cell phone. How stupid was that? Now I had to get a new laptop, email account, and cell phone. Of course, I should have had these all along.

Because I wanted to be as productive as possible as soon as possible, this felt like an urgent and daunting undertaking. Setting up my home office felt as overwhelming as it can feel to learn new technology in a new job. On the Monday following D-Day Thursday, after many weekend hours at electronics and wireless phone stores, I had a new laptop and cell phone. I had conquered the first of many challenges.

When I fired up my new laptop for the first time, I unknowingly selected security settings that made it like getting into the Pentagon every time I logged on. I had to enter two passwords before even booting up. After more than three hours on the phone with a local support person, a computer wizard from someplace else in the world reconstructed reasonable security settings.

Next, I had to get my Microsoft Outlook account to sync my emails, contacts, and calendar between my computer and cell phone like I was used to. Without access to the company help desk, I paid an independent computer consultant to get my technology working right. It was comforting once my new environment was close to what I had at the company. This was a small but important win to appreciate each day I used my new devices.

And then I had to change my user names and email addresses for my online accounts. But you have to *remember* your login information to do this. After working on this for days, I *still* came across account profiles I had to change. How can anyone possibly remember all their user names, passwords, and ridiculous security questions—including some that convince you big brother is watching? How do "they" know things about me I never entered into any computer? Scary!

☑ **TIP: Set up your new home technology similar to your previous company setup and hire a "computer geek."** While dealing with so many other changes, the fewer new operating systems and software programs you have to learn during this stressful time, the better. Pay close attention when setting up your security profile on a new computer. If you're not tech-savvy, consider paying an expert.

☑ **TIP: Separate business and personal devices and data.** More companies are using a Bring Your Own Device (BYOD) approach for cell phones, tablets, etc. After recovering from not having my own laptop and cell phone, and later experiencing BYOD practices, I would never go back to using only company-owned devices.

While ensuring compliance with company policies, be deliberate and cautious about the devices and email accounts you use, where you store your data (emails, contacts, and calendars), and how you can retain access to the information if you leave your company for any reason.

Driving to the Dark Side

Venturing out one afternoon to meet a friend, being alone in my car awakened deep, dark thoughts and feelings about what happened. A desolate image of floating in the ocean, alone on a life raft, was a small taste of the emotional tsunami to come.

When this despair hit, I realized I had focused so much energy on setting up my home office to avoid this dark place. The busier I was, the less likely I was to fold up like a tent, unable to get out of bed. Working on my transition at a frenetic pace over the next several months was, in part, my attempt to avoid a decline into deep depression.

Feeling Empowered

It was time to read and understand my separation documents and decide if I would hire attorney. After a closer read, I scheduled a consultation for the next morning and retained the lawyer's services.

Working with my attorney gave me a glimmer of positive feelings. I didn't yield to self-imposed expectations to be a good employee who returned signed documents with no changes. Not so fast! It was more important to be 100% comfortable with what I signed than it was to sign it quickly.

Reviewing the details with my attorney provided an important sense of empowerment during this difficult time. It reminded me that I was a smart and capable professional with many transferable skills.

Whether or not you hire an attorney, below are generic things to look for in separation documents:

- Be clear and comfortable about the time the company gave you to sign document(s). Thirty to 45 days from receipt is a reasonable timeframe in which to consult an attorney and complete other research.

- If your position was eliminated, be sure this is stated as the reason for your separation. Rather than leaving a position voluntarily or due to performance issues, job elimination might make you eligible for better separation terms, and qualifies you for unemployment compensation.

- Include a clause that prohibits the company from denying unemployment claims.

- Ensure the stipulations in your signed agreement cannot be changed. If it exists, get a copy of the ERISA-filed separation plan. This could be a controlling document that supersedes the signed agreement and allows future changes.

- Change one-sided non-disparagement clauses to be mutual.

- If the employer offered company-paid outplacement services from a specific firm, consider asking for the monetary value so you can select your own coach. If they did not include outplacement services, you could request a company-paid program or funds to hire your own career coach. Researching local coaches and fees is one reason you might need time to sign your document(s).

- Don't bother requesting a letter of recommendation from anyone you worked for or with who is still at the company. Other than confirming your titles and dates of employment, most companies prohibit substantive professional references.

☑ **TIP: Consult with an attorney qualified in employment law.** Other than the basic acknowledgement of receipt, consult with an attorney before signing separation documents. It's more important to protect your interests than it is to sign and submit documents quickly.

Shower Party for the Twisted Sister

In the shower, where I've always done some of my best think-ing, I found myself in a new, happy place about my whole situation.

In years past, I often thought about someday creating a combination of satisfying freelance and consulting work—maybe at the same company and other places. I realized I had a remarkable opportunity to figure this out with help from an expert career coach. I could reinvent my career into something even more rewarding and satisfying than my pre-vious position.

With this new perspective, I danced instead of cried in the shower. While still in this happy place, I called my sister and gave myself a new nickname: *Twisted Sister*. My state of mind flipped dramatically from feeling up and optimistic about the possibilities ahead, to depressed or angry—yelling, crying, and stomping my feet.

On this day, my husband came home to a different person—an unexpectedly happy one. Everyone, including me, was sur-prised I had gotten there in one week. But, as expected so early in my transition, I didn't stay in that place for long. It was great while it lasted—and I knew I would be back as time went on.

Melting Down and Gearing Up

With fortunate timing, I had had just enough time to get or-ganized at home before taking a short trip. We visited my mother in the New York area and attended a family wedding in the Boston area. Given everything I accomplished during the past week, I was ready to take a break, then come home and begin the hard work of my transition. As challenging as it was to get my technology set up, I knew that had been the easy part.

Trying (unsuccessfully) to keep things in perspective, I reminded myself often that nobody close had died or become terminally ill. I had not been deployed to a war zone or lost a limb. But my brother-in-law shared his opinion that job loss could produce effects similar to post-traumatic stress disorder (PTSD). My reactions included flashbacks to what happened *that day,* extreme highs and lows, and intense rage over minor incidents. This could explain my volatile temper tantrums in response to the smallest frustrations.

While enjoying time with family during this trip, a small incident brought me to my knees. A strong paranoid reaction to a relatively small frustration triggered an emotional meltdown and more intense depression than I had felt in years.

Here's what happened. Emails I sent to two people at my previous company bounced back with an alert message that my new email address was rejected by the server. My immediate conclusion was that the company had blacklisted and blocked me from sending emails through their server. This irrational thought kept me up all night and made me sick in intestinal ways that need no further explanation. The next morning, emails to people outside the company also got rejected. The problem was with my internet provider, not the company server. Now why didn't I figure *that* out sooner?

Unfortunately, I couldn't shake the negative thoughts and numbing depression that washed over me through the rest of the weekend and into Tuesday. Where was that happier place I had found in the shower last week? Of course, it was too soon to stay there for extended periods.

Insights: Emotional Responses to Loss

It's helpful to know you're not alone as you deal with the emotional impact of a life-shattering event. Give yourself time to be with the experience, and then to heal with reasonable expectations about how long it might take to rebuild resilience that sticks.

Suffering a significant loss of any type can set off a grieving reaction. It's common to experience the five stages of grief identified by psychiatrist Elisabeth Kübler-Ross. Losing my job after 20 years was a trauma I needed to mourn and recover from before I could reinvent my professional identity.

More recent research suggests that, rather than moving from stage one to stage five in a linear fashion, people go back and forth through these stages repeatedly. I experienced several visits to each stage:

1. **Denial.** Before D-Day, I fooled myself into believing I wouldn't lose my job. After the initial shock, I wondered if the company might offer to bring me back as a consultant to help transition my work to others. Deep down, I knew such an offer was unlikely, and I probably wouldn't accept it anyway.

2. **Anger.** In recurring visits to this stage, both on and long after D-Day, I experienced anger about what had happened.

3. **Bargaining.** Rather than total job elimination, I wondered why management hadn't considered changing part of my job to a consulting contract.

4. **Depression.** I had multiple emotional meltdowns to this rock-bottom place. At the lowest points, I felt helpless

and hopeless about my ability to make things better. Besides seeking therapy, it was important to seize moments when I felt resilient enough to take actions to change my situation.

5. **Acceptance.** I arrived and stayed here more often as I healed, worked hard, and created new opportunities.

A related concept is in one of my favorite books called *Bend, Not Break: A Life in Two Worlds*, by Ping Fu with MeiMei Fox. Quoted from the epilogue with permission: "There are three types of holes in topology. A tunnel has two openings that connect to the outside. A pocket has only one opening. And a void, an enclosed space like the inside of a ball, has no connection to the outside world ... It is in tunnels that we start our journey; in pockets that our imagination blossoms toward the opening; and in voids that we must face our naked, agonizing vulnerability."

Losing my job felt mostly like a tunnel I needed to travel through to get to the other side. My worst times felt more like a void with no way out, and my triumph felt like blossoming out of a pocket toward a new way of life. I hope you, too, find guidance and inspiration in these concepts related to loss.

Lunch for the Inmate Who's Pulling Out Her Hair

This was another day of refining my technology set up and following up to continue health insurance benefits through COBRA. My PTSD and hair-trigger response to frustration struck again as I dealt with confusion and anxiety about the costs and timing to secure health benefits without interruption.

As frustrating as dealing with COBRA, nearly two weeks after D-Day, I still didn't have my contacts in Microsoft Outlook on my new laptop and cell phone. These were an essential gold mine for my transition. I could transfer them from my old company phone to my new phone, but I couldn't download them to my laptop. After the company sent them on a CD, the data got corrupted and disappeared the first time I accessed it. Can you imagine the words that came out of my mouth when that happened?

A few days later, my favorite help desk technician from the company had permission to download the contacts to my laptop through a remote connection. Once the information was secured on my new devices, I returned the company phone I had held onto like a life raft. And finally, with assistance from several new technology wizards, my Outlook emails, contacts, and calendar were syncing perfectly between my laptop and phone—a major relief!

On several days before my technology issues were resolved, my husband came home for lunch to a screaming banshee, almost literally pulling out her hair. After more than 20 years of marital bliss, he knew nobody could help me when I was in this wicked state of anger and frustration.

Being so wrapped up in my own angst made it easy to forget how my husband was also negatively affected by my job loss. All he could do was leave a lunch tray for the "inmate," hoping she would eat. Yes, I would eat food put in front of me, but I wouldn't take time out to prepare it for myself.

My strong need to feel a sense of control drove me to focus intense energy on my search. As long as there was transition work to do—which was endless—I felt obsessed to keep working.

Career Coaching Begins

Having access to excellent career coaching services seemed like one of the best things about my whole situation.

As a Hard-to-Define Professional, returning to the job market after 20 years in a one-of-a-kind role, I expected this transition to take quite a while. In fact, I made the conscious decision to not rush to find a new job. Rather than a sense of urgency to land quickly, I planned to take my time to figure out what I wanted to do and how to make it happen.

In retrospect, my coach might have been accustomed to working with clients in clearly defined professions, eager to land new jobs as quickly as possible. My sense of the journey I was embarking on might have been clearer than my coach's. During an initial call, I expressed concerns about sustaining the motivation and fortitude I needed for my transition. I was afraid my lack of urgency to find a job might bring on depression, making it hard to get out of bed to do anything.

We worked together behind the scenes for several weeks. I needed this time to get emotionally and otherwise prepared to interact with professional contacts. It was interesting to note who from my previous company contacted me during this time, and painful to not hear from people I had worked with for years.

Fortunately, my previous boss (the retired chairman) offered to be a professional reference. When he called at the end of the second week, I cried the moment I heard his voice. This was a clear indication I wasn't ready to network with professional contacts.

In contrast to concerns about being too depressed to function, I wasn't sure where so much productive energy came from. But I wanted to capitalize on it as long as it was with me. My mother always said I had two speeds—fast and stop. At D-Day plus two weeks, I was operating in overdrive, often to the point of total exhaustion.

I knew I needed to balance getting a lot of work done *and* taking time to relax and enjoy my freedom. It became a missed opportunity to do many things: take better care of myself; nurture my creative side; enjoy hobbies (read, study Spanish, exercise); and pursue things I wanted to do for a long time but hadn't (yoga, warm water exercise classes, a writers' workshop, cooking with my husband).

Unfortunately, most of these good intentions didn't happen because I continued obsessive work on my transition. Some people I met while networking shared this intense focus on their search. Others had a hard time focusing on it, easily distracted by domestic obligations or enjoyable things they would rather do. These ways of dealing with the situation are not right or wrong—just different.

After working through my acute hurt and angry feelings with my coach, I needed ample time to prepare for my search. I had to explore and articulate my professional value proposition and learn how to market myself to potential employers, recruiters, and clients. Some would call this professional branding. I thought of it as reinventing myself.

I was confident my coach and others at the outplacement firm would help me work through my career transition in these ways:

- Deal with emotional turmoil and get in a frame of mind to network and interview
- Explain why I no longer had a job
- Explore possibilities and define what I did and didn't want to do in my next job(s)
- Discover, articulate, and market my value proposition
- Develop a LinkedIn profile and new résumé

- Learn how to use the internet and social media to network and pursue opportunities
- Determine who, when, and how to ask for professional references
- Prepare for and debrief interviews
- Negotiate job offers
- Land in one or more new places as a reinvented professional

Rome wasn't built in a day, and I wasn't professionally reinvented in weeks, or even months—it took a year to create my new direction. My transformation involved many dead ends, meltdowns, and directional shifts, with important victories along the way. I was happy to have a capable and compassionate coach by my side as I began this marathon.

 ## Insights: Outplacement and Career Coaching

Some outplacement firms offer primarily group sessions that mix clients from different professional levels. Others emphasize working one-on-one with a dedicated coach. Complementing standard career transition tools, each outplacement firm or individual coach might provide unique methods and guidance. Some coaches make introductions on your behalf.

During conversations with others in transition, it was common for clients to express frustration about not getting the value they expected from their outplacement or coaching experiences. Some natural tension is to be expected in many productive coaching relationships. This is especially true for endeavors that are inherently challenging, with many ups and downs. If your coach isn't helping you go places you wouldn't go on your own, he or she might not be giving you what you need. However, pushing too far or too fast could be counterproductive.

With most things in life, you get out of them as much as you put in to them. Intending to squeeze every drop of value I could out of the process, I did my transition work to the fullest extent possible, and got tremendous benefits from my experience.

 TIP: Consider options to hire your own coach. If given the option, consider receiving the monetary value instead of a specific outplacement program or coach. This allows you to hire someone based on research or referrals from people you trust. You could interview a few coaches and select one you think can best help you.

If you have a choice, select someone who combines high-level transition strategies with tactical search methods. It's a bonus if they have a strong professional network and make introductions on your behalf.

Insights: Analyzing What Happened, Why, and Where to Go From Here

Losing a job could raise questions in your mind about how your performance contributed to losing your seat. My job loss led me to also wonder what questions other people might have about what was wrong with my performance.

Whenever something troubling happens, my strong tendency is to focus on what I might have done to cause the problem. With introspection, I can always find reasons to criticize myself. Please pardon this generalization, but I've seen more females look inward and blame themselves for problems, and more males look outward—getting angry or blaming others when things go wrong. Of course, this isn't always the case.

As my own worst critic, I considered ways I might have contributed to the decision to eliminate my job. In my self-blaming mode, I wondered if I should have sought more assignments, even if I didn't want to do them. In my self-supporting mode, I knew it was not about me, and believed my job was eliminated for reasons that had nothing to do with my performance.

During strong economic periods, and before the Global financial crisis impacted jobs, it was common for people to wonder how individuals contributed to losing their seat at the table. As millions lost their jobs during and after 2008, it seemed more widely understood that anyone could lose one or more jobs for reasons totally unrelated to their performance. As my unemployed status continued for more than a year, I met hundreds of professionals in transition. My previous bias to assign personal responsibility for job loss receded further into the abyss.

Without dwelling on harsh self-criticism, it could be beneficial to study and learn from things that happened and take these lessons into the future. But, rather than dissecting what I had done wrong to cause the separation, it became more important to discover what I wanted to do, and then create the next phase of my career and my life.

Career Coaching Assignments

Eager to dig in and complete the first assignments from my coach, I sometimes felt overwhelmed by the work. My first three self-discovery assignments are described below. These and other methods and tools I found most and least helpful are expanded upon in the 25 Activities section.

1. **Myers Briggs Type Inventory (MBTI).** This instrument is designed to help you understand your preferred styles for interacting with others, processing information, making decisions, and dealing with the world.

   I always resist taking the MBTI because I don't like pigeonholing myself into one answer for each question. As I read each statement about preferring A or B, my inner voice says, *Well, it depends on the situation.* While I like to believe I'm flexible and situational in how I interact with the world around me, my "ISTJ" profile (Introversion, Sensing, Thinking, Judging) is the same every time I take the assessment.

   My coach planned to use my MBTI report to get to know me better in the context of my professional behaviors and preferences. Given my tendency toward introspection and self-discovery, my coach asked me to review my report and share these insights:
   - What did and didn't fit with how I saw myself
   - Key takeaways for me to work on
   - Things my coach needed to know about me to be most helpful

   My profile remained the same, but my Introvert (I) score hit the maximum value and was higher than ever. This was consistent with feeling like an injured animal that needed to retreat and lick its wounds. Also in sync with my profile, I spent three hours analyzing my report, and sent a two-page chart that summarized what I discovered about myself and how my coach could best help me.

2. **Important Work Factors.** Several worksheets helped me think about my ideal role and work environment. Based on my entire journey, I created a comprehensive worksheet to help you explore and discover what's most important and compelling as you pursue your next chapter (Sample 1: Self-Discovery for Inventive Career Transitions).

3. **Accomplishment Stories: Problem/Actions/Results/Skills (PARS).** This assignment required me to describe my professional accomplishments. My coach asked me to develop a dozen one-page success stories. This standard assignment has a few different names, all serving the same purpose. The intention was to use my PARS to fuel my new résumé and LinkedIn profile, networking activities, and responses to interview questions.

As an individual contributor in staff rather than line management roles, it required extra creativity to attribute quantifiable, bottom-line results to my accomplishments. In the end, I was pleased with these documents.

⊘ **TIP: Take stock of your past accomplishments.** It's never too soon to list things you accomplished in your previous positions. Besides input for your upcoming job search, recalling your achievements helps you bounce back if you are doubting your capabilities.

⊘ **TIP: Take one step at a time and keep notes on things you'll get to when you're ready.** Working on your transition can feel overwhelming. The longer you've been out of the job market, the more overwhelming it's likely to be. Write down early ideas about possible future jobs, personal and professional connections, potential references, etc. You'll get to them when you're ready.

☑ **TIP: Subscribe to daily career resources or other inspirations.** Select content that informs and motivates you to tackle what lies ahead. Daily emails from Work It Daily.com (formerly careerealism.com) included short articles with inspirational and practical tips for many aspects of a job search. Reading applicable articles was a great way to start each morning.

Two Weeks of Big Accomplishments
At the end of two weeks, I stepped back to pat myself on the back for all I had accomplished in such a short time:

- Set myself up to work at home
- Started career coaching assignments
- Gained a new appreciation for how much I would benefit from others' guidance as things progressed

Intellectually, I knew I needed to pace myself to prevent burnout. Behaviorally, I couldn't walk away from my computer until I was too tired to think straight. Besides working on transition assignments, I enjoyed writing journal entries whenever I had time. As ideas relentlessly popped into my head, I jotted them down and couldn't wait to get them into the document.

☑ **TIP: Recognize every success along the way.** No success is too small to acknowledge as something you achieved because you are a capable professional. And celebrate the bigger things you achieve in bigger ways.

Seeing the Bright Side

Getting ready for my second coaching session, as fast as the shower water, words flowed into my head for my journal. I began week three in a better place with fewer trips to the dark side. More than looking backward to how hurt and angry I felt about what happened, I was looking forward to new opportunities. My coach gave me three assignments for the following week:

1. **Résumé.** My first step was to update my contact information and most recent job. A few weeks later, my coach would provide samples of strong résumés and help me use my other assignments to create the new version.

2. **LinkedIn.** After setting up a bare-bones profile, I attended a free one-hour webinar presented by LinkedIn. This was a prerequisite to attend a "LinkedIn for Job Seekers" seminar at my outplacement firm.

3. **Departure Statement.** This standard job search tool is a brief, carefully crafted response to questions about why you are no longer in your previous job (Activity 4: Departure Statement).

The Total Package

I asked my coach questions about presenting myself in interviews and networking meetings. Here are factors to consider:

Clothing. Despite the prevalence of casual work environments, unless someone tells you otherwise, err on the side of business attire for interviews and networking. My wardrobe had become quite casual (and mostly black), so I added tailored jackets and flattering colors.

Hair. A neat and clean hairstyle should be more important than what color it is. Wanting my hairstyle to look like Jamie Lee Curtis, I had no plans to cover my increasing gray. PART III includes insights about midlife career transitions and age biases.

Facial Expressions. Ask someone you trust about facial expressions you might not be aware of. Videotape and discuss a mock interview with someone who gives you candid feedback. If you don't have a career coach, find someone at a local networking meeting to help you with this.

True confession: I have deep vertical ("11") lines between my eyebrows. Even when I'm most relaxed, they never disappear, and they get more pronounced as I age. People often think I'm angry or scowling when I'm simply listening or concentrating. Despite misinterpretations of my facial expressions, I tried Botox but passed on additional rounds of poison and pain. I wished someone would invent a virtual reality version of Photoshop.

Weight. Many people try to lose weight to avoid potential biases and discrimination by interviewers. Your relationship with food could make this easier or harder during this stressful time. Regardless of your weight, present a neat, professional appearance.

Voice. Phone interviews were the most frequent initial screening method during my search. They were also common for interviews with hiring managers. Knowing colleagues didn't always take me seriously until we worked together, I consciously fortified my childlike voice during calls and meetings.

⊘ **TIP: Make coaching sessions work for you.** Coaching sessions are your opportunity to get the help you need. In addition to whatever your coach thinks you need to discuss, keep a running list of topics and questions you want to address.

⊘ **TIP: Manage your time your way.** Use time in ways that work best for you. In the early weeks, I focused on self-discovery, research, and planning upcoming search activities. To wake up my brain, I did simple administrative tasks for the first hour, and then dove into more challenging work.

Initially, I aimed to be out of the house for meetings and errands two days a week and work at home the other three (make that five) days. Once I felt ready for prime time, I hoped the number of days out of the house would increase to at least three.

Silver Linings List

Three weeks after D-Day, I felt happier than I had in a long time. To capture my positive sentiments, I created a list of great things that probably wouldn't have happened if I hadn't lost my job—things worth celebrating:

- Extra time and energy to pursue new interests
- Enriched relationships with family and friends

- Expert coaching assistance
- Opportunity to find satisfying work
- A new laptop and cell phone
- No more 35-mile, hour-long commutes (each way); saving on gas, tolls, wear and tear on my car, and auto insurance premiums, not to mention reducing my carbon footprint
- Working at home in my pajamas
- Flexibility to schedule medical appointments, haircuts, house repairs, and social outings with friends
- Time to take better care of myself and shed extra pounds with healthier food and exercise

Unfortunately, rather than improving my diet and exercising more, my job search and writing took over. Taking care of me fell to the bottom of the list and I gained weight. This needed attention when I could get myself there.

✅ **TIP: Create a Silver Linings List.** Take stock and remind yourself of the positive aspects of your transition—advantages you would not have if you had stayed in your job.

✅ **TIP: Balance working hard with relaxing.** Take advantage of this opportunity to balance working hard on your transition with taking time to smell the roses. Do things you haven't had time for while working full time. Nurture relationships you might have taken for granted or would like to enrich.

Finding balance is easier for people who can walk away from work to take much-needed breaks. My husband enjoyed many afternoon bike rides during his transition. For those of us who are financially or otherwise driven to find our next jobs, a search can be all-consuming. My irresistible drive to keep working made it seem impossible to listen to my own guidance to leave my computer.

Reality Sets In and Hard Work Begins

Four weeks into my transition, thinking about D-Day triggered hurt and anger that took me back to the dark place. It was a scary dose of reality when I paid bills for the first time in the context of no income. This motivated me to work through initial steps to prepare for my search.

A colleague who lost her job on D-Day started a new job two weeks later. Her expertise and target roles were more clearly defined, and she was eager to get a new job right away. Her landing reminded me that I had to make this happen for me. However, I had more background work to do, I wasn't in a rush, and I was confident it would happen when I was ready.

Career Coaching Session 3

My coach and I discussed taking more time to sharpen my value proposition and marketing materials before I would be ready to network and apply for jobs. We also talked about the possibility I could end up with a few combined work situations, such as full-time employment, part-time contracts, and/or freelance projects.

After meeting with my coach, I attended a seminar at the outplacement firm on using LinkedIn to research and target potential employers. I was both excited and apprehensive about leveraging this platform as one of the most essential and powerful resources for job seekers.

My assignments for the next two weeks were to flesh out my LinkedIn profile and draft my new résumé. The primary sources for ideas on how to market myself were job postings for the kinds of positions I might pursue and LinkedIn profile summaries I admired.

Another Sleep-Challenged Night

Not my usual time to be at my computer, I wrote several pages in my journal between 1:30-3:30 a.m.

Both surprising and overwhelming, I found quite a few job postings on LinkedIn that matched my skills and interests. Because I wanted to continue as an individual contributor without direct reports, some were at a higher or broader level of responsibility than I was seeking.

As interesting as some jobs were, I had to crawl and then walk before I could run back into the job market. Still just exploring possibilities, my marketing story and documents were not far enough along to apply for attractive jobs I found.

Sharpening My Professional Value Proposition: Taking Time to Get this Right

To flesh out my LinkedIn summary and craft the top sections of my résumé, I compiled and grouped four pages (yikes!) of strengths and transferable skills. Despite great source material, writing my new résumé felt like an impossible challenge that made my accomplishment stories seem easy.

The work to clearly define and articulate my value proposition was challenging and anxiety provoking. It was also mission-critical for the next phase of my search. I kept reminding myself that if anybody could play with words and phrases to fuel a résumé and LinkedIn summary, it was me. Was I having fun yet? Not so much, but at least this work gave me several days to stay at home in my pajamas.

While working on describing myself, I received a snail-mail letter inviting me to select my recognition gift for 20 years of service at my former company. I guess someone forgot to take me out of the system that administered this process.

Receiving messages of appreciation for my dedication and contributions to the company made my stomach flip. Once I got past my gut instinct to shred the letter, I proudly went on-line to select a gift. After all, who couldn't use a Swiss Army knife (how fitting) and binoculars?

⊘ **TIP: Use available resources to learn how to market you.** Articulating your expertise and strengths is one of your most critical transition activities. The most valuable resources for crafting the top sections of your résumé and LinkedIn profile are online job postings that match what you *can* and *want* to do next. This is an essential element of the Sweet Spot Job Search Method and Activity 3: Online Job Searches and Daily Alerts.

Month 2: Discovery
Learning to Market "Me, Inc."

Monday Mitzvah and "Ladies Who Lunch"

For a Yiddish-to-English translation, a mitzvah is a kind and considerate deed performed with a joyous heart. On this note, I took a friend to a medical procedure at an outpatient surgical center (you know, that 50th birthday present that keeps on giving every 5 to 10 years). It was fulfilling to take the day to be there for her and enrich our friendship.

Her procedure was uneventful and we enjoyed a late lunch afterwards. As it turned into a full day away from my computer, I had to convince myself it was okay. New entries on my Silver Linings List were the ability to be there for my friend and to enjoy a whole day out of my office (and pajamas).

Antsy Nancy Gets Back to Work

It was time to focus on my résumé. Source materials included accomplishment stories, transferable skills, key words and phrases from job postings, and action verbs. Diving into the challenge, I struggled to keep negative thoughts at bay. I still had significant work to do before I was packaged well enough to put myself out there. Sometimes I felt like an impatient racehorse preparing to charge out of my gate, but I knew I wasn't ready.

I explored daily job postings on LinkedIn, Indeed, and SimplyHired. Indeed consolidates postings from multiple sources and became my most valuable source for jobs to apply for.

LinkedIn Profile

In addition to my résumé, fleshing out my LinkedIn profile would be my focus for the next few weeks. I expanded my profile summary, work experience, education, and skills. It was challenging to create a summary that came across as confident and competent, but not boastful and arrogant. Not wanting to sound egotistical, I reworked several early versions.

I hoped to get feedback in my next coaching session to finalize my résumé and LinkedIn summary. At this point, finalized meant good enough to road test for job applications and networking. I knew I would refine them continually as I found examples I liked and learned from what was and wasn't working. This became quite an understatement.

⊘ **TIP: Master LinkedIn Privacy Settings.** Actively manage your privacy and security settings. For example, as you create and edit your profile, keep it private so your connections don't receive notices every time you change anything—even one comma. Remain anonymous as you explore other profiles before making yours public. Don't unlock your visibility until your profile is ready for connections, potential employers, and recruiters to see (Activity 8: LinkedIn Profile and Connections).

⊘ **TIP: Leverage free resources and consider hiring a professional.** Take advantage of free programs or paid professionals to write your LinkedIn profile and résumé. Whether or not you hire someone, you can learn best practices by attending local career management seminars and networking groups for job seekers. You might find these in your local library or meetup groups. Many are free or low cost.

Who *Am* I?

My sister-in-law is a senior HR executive who had experienced a difficult job loss. She provided helpful (and hard-to-hear) feedback on the umpteenth draft of my résumé and profile. Unfortunately, I *still* had not clearly explained who I was professionally or what kind role I was looking for. She said a recruiter or potential employer could read my documents and not understand what I had done, could do, or wanted to do.

Crap! I had a *lot* more work to do. Discouraged but determined, my résumé and LinkedIn revisions continued far into the future. Eventually, my résumés kicked butt and got to the top of the "Yes" pile for interviews (Samples 2-A, 2-B).

Words, Words, and More Words

Losing sleep and spending hours at my computer, I drowned in thousands of edits and versions of my documents. My obsession with perfection just wouldn't quit.

My husband worried about my not getting out of my pajamas and leaving the house. I was spinning my wheels and depression was creeping in. I knew I needed more variety and balance in how I spent my time. Thinking this would come when I was ready, I also sensed I might need to push myself there.

I'm Ready for My Close-Up,
But I Still Don't Know Who I Am

Words, words, and more words—but words that created clarity were still missing!

My Monday-Mitzvah friend is a talented conceptual artist and photographer and she offered to take my picture for

LinkedIn. Wearing a red suit jacket added pop to my image, and I was happy with the photo I posted. (I replaced it later with a studio portrait taken for this book.)

Career Coaching Session 4

With new versions of my résumé and profile in hand, my coach echoed my sister-in-law's feedback—I *still* had not crystallized my distinct professional brand or value proposition. We discussed ideas I would continue to play with.

Even though my documents weren't fully baked, my coach and I agreed on two jobs worth applying for. Unfortunately, when I went online, both were closed to new applicants. I planned to include these companies on my yet-to-be-developed target list.

We also agreed I would send a letter of interest to a management consulting firm that had piqued my curiosity. After searching LinkedIn for people who worked at the firm, I addressed a letter to someone who might have been involved in hiring decisions for roles that interested me. Besides requesting an exploratory call with her, I applied for a copywriter position on the company's website. Because I was intrigued by this firm, I thought I would approach people there from multiple angles over time. Stay tuned for more on this later.

My next coaching assignment was to develop my elevator pitch for networking and interviews. My task was to draft five minutes of material that could be pared down to three minutes or 90 seconds to fit the situation. I hoped this would help me clearly define what I had done and wanted to do. I also expected this work to lead to further revisions on my résumé and LinkedIn profile.

Birthday Banshee and Champing at the Bit

With additional feedback on my documents, I was more frustrated than I realized. Tired, hungry, and overwhelmed by how much work I wanted to get done, I had a major meltdown when I got home from my fourth coaching session. My evil twin made an unwelcome guest appearance, and my husband almost didn't come home for dinner. Hey—it was my birthday and it should have been a good day!

With a strong need to vent, I wrote about why I was frustrated with my transition process. The issues I struggled with might provide insights as you navigate similar questions and challenges.

1. **Defining my profession.** My coach tried to help me define my professional identity as something specific, such as communications. This was challenging for several reasons:
   - My professional experience was Hard-to-Define
   - I didn't know what I *could* or *wanted* to do next
   - I wanted to explore several directions
   - I believed I needed to market myself in a multi-faceted vs. pigeonholed way

2. **Being open to working anywhere.** While trying to help me be *more* specific about what I had done and wanted to do, my coach suggested I remain more open and *less* specific about the companies I targeted. I wanted to focus on small- to mid-size management consulting firms. My coach urged me to also target corporate jobs—especially in financial services and large companies.

3. **Positioning myself to stay within my recent industry.** My coach advised that my LinkedIn profile should list Financial Services as my industry because it was where I had been for

20 years and, therefore, the only category that would make sense to employers and recruiters.

In contrast, I chose Management Consulting as my industry because it was my targeted direction. I believed selecting an industry that accurately reflected work I had done and wanted to do was the best option and 100% credible.

My coach and others believed getting a job in financial services was my path of least resistance. This concerned me for several reasons:

- My last job would be difficult to replicate in any company, including financial services.
- My role focused more on processes than technical business content. I had broad exposure to the whole business, but I didn't have deep technical expertise in financial services.
- Working at another financial services company was low on my list of what I wanted to do. While financial service companies can be purpose-driven, I wanted to find work I cared about—a lot.

4. **Still not being ready to put myself out there.** I thought I would be ready to reach out to professional contacts by this time in my transition. I was eager to contact people in management consulting firms. My coach didn't think I was ready. Despite these frustrations, I accomplished three important things by the end of this day:

- Emailed draft bullets for my previous boss to consider including in a LinkedIn recommendation—sure to be one of my most powerful assets
- Sent my first general approach letter to the management consulting firm I was interested in
- Sent revised documents to my coach, hoping for final feedback before I used them

Churning Words, Gaining Clarity, Still Champing at the Bit

After two more days of endless revisions to my résumé, LinkedIn profile, and elevator pitch, I thought (hoped) I was close to articulating a clear story. By the end of the following week, I wanted to reach out to key contacts in my primary area of interest (small- to mid-size management consulting firms). My plan was to reality test the opportunity I was looking for and identify other people to contact. Search Strategy #2 describes the type of role and company I was most interested in.

At D-Day plus six weeks, I wanted to be ready for prime time. My inner racehorse couldn't wait to charge out of the gate.

LinkedIn Profile: Getting to "All-Star" Strength

Continuing to build my LinkedIn profile and connections, I invited several alumni from my former company to connect, endorsed some of their skills and asked them to return the favor, and asked four additional people for recommendations. My fingers were crossed that they would come through, but I expected these to require care and feeding to complete over the next few weeks. These additions would elevate my profile strength from "Expert" to "All-Star."

First Job Application on LinkedIn

A job I had wanted to apply for the previous week was re-posted two hours before I logged on to LinkedIn. It was at a small consulting firm focused on employee and customer engagement—areas of strong interest. At 5:30 p.m., I sent my résumé, cover letter, and a memorable customer experience story to the founder and CEO. Thinking I might be a match for the job, I was eager to see if I would get a response.

Oh shit! Two hours after I hit "Send," I found a *big* mistake in my cover letter! Exhausted when I wrote the letter, I used a different (but similar) company name in my closing paragraph. Because I wasn't on a Microsoft Exchange account, I couldn't recall and resend the email. So I sent a new one with a p.s., practically begging the CEO to disregard and forgive my error. It was unfortunate that he was the designated recipient. I probably blew *any* chance to land a job at this company.

Lesson learned. Especially with Friday afternoon and weekend job postings, submitting a 100% accurate document early Monday morning is far better than sending it with errors Friday night or during the weekend. I had to resist visceral (OCD?) urges to submit applications as soon as they were done—urges that were clearly irrational because nobody would see what I submitted until at least Monday.

While submitting superior, error-free documents rules, speed is also important. Applying right after a job is posted can have a significant positive impact on rising to the top of the "Yes" pile. With self-imposed pressure, I aimed to apply within 24 hours at most, and within a few hours on weekdays. Once my résumés rocked, numerous quick submissions resulted in calls and interviews soon after I sent them—some within hours.

Weeks after applying for this job with an imperfect letter, I was introduced to and met with a senior executive who was about to leave this firm. Over time, I became less interested in the firm, and he became one of my most valued networking connections.

✅ **TIP: Accuracy trumps speed in job applications.** Don't send anything, especially résumés and cover letters, when you're tired. When I rushed to submit letters and résumés, I often found errors or edits the next time I read them. Particularly during evenings and weekends, let them sit overnight for another read in the morning!

I'm Not a Plug 'N Play Widget

Spending *many* hours at my laptop, I continued refining my résumé and one-page networking profile that included a list of target companies. Based on common advice to not provide a résumé until asked, the profile would be used during networking meetings to explain my capabilities, what I wanted to do, and where I wanted to work.

Several people thought my résumé should include a statement about the role I was looking for. I later learned that résumé best practices no longer include a professional objective stating the type of position you are seeking. Still necessary in conversations, it seemed impossible to describe my expertise and what I wanted to do. I was grappling with being a Hard-to-Define Professional—not a plug 'n play widget.

My perfectionism prevailed while making endless changes to my résumé and other documents. As I incorporated ideas from online job postings and impressive LinkedIn profiles, new thinking gradually emerged about how I might describe and market myself. This became clearer as I developed several search strategies.

Month 3: Reentry
Ready or Not, Running Out of the Gate

As I zeroed in on my strongest interest—internal services roles in consulting firms—my coach reminded me to pursue two or three simultaneous search directions. When urged to apply for financial services positions like the one I lost, I reiterated that those jobs were one-of-a-kind and rarely posted.

Using various iterations of my résumé, I applied for six jobs on LinkedIn and other job sites. Several required completion of online applications; some accepted a cover letter and/or résumé. Using a recommended format, I customized a letter for each job. They included a two-column chart, showing key requirements of the job on the left and how I could meet those requirements on the right. I later abandoned this format because it generated fewer (if any) responses than letters using paragraphs and bullets.

Two applications were rejected immediately through automated Applicant Tracking Systems. I was not surprised, and knew a lot more of this would happen.

It was time to follow up on the exploratory letter I sent to the consulting firm I was interested in. This felt like a big step, and I was nervous about making the call. I got reacquainted with the procrastinator who visits me when I'm most anxious about something I have to do.

When I finally made the call, the conversation confirmed that I needed more practice responding when someone asked me to tell them about myself. Even with all the work I had done during the past several weeks, it wasn't easy to describe my experience, capabilities, and search objective.

We explored a few roles at the firm. This included a brief conversation about the copywriter position I had applied for, which seemed too junior. Even though it wasn't what I was looking for, she encouraged me to complete a second online application for a consulting position. While neither role was a match, she would keep me in mind for potential opportunities and possible meetings with principals of the firm.

✓ **TIP: Practice networking and hone your elevator pitch with friends, family, and casual network connections.** Expect to stumble through early introductions and interviews that happen before you're ready. Practice with people who are less significant in your search before you go after high-stakes networking and interviewing for positions you really want.

✓ **TIP: Sound clear, concise, and natural vs. stiff and scripted.** Refine your elevator pitch and responses to sound clear and conversational. Sounding over-rehearsed can backfire, especially with executive recruiters. I found it challenging to put words on paper that came out of my mouth sounding like how I normally speak.

Networking Workshop and Career Coaching Session 7

I attended a workshop on using LinkedIn and other sources to develop a list of target companies. The instructor showed us an example of a full-page, single-spaced list of hospitals and said we needed to do extensive research to develop a long list of target companies. When clients met with coaches in the outplacement firm, they wanted us to explain why each company was on our list.

After the session, I felt unsettled and intimidated by this approach. As a Hard-to-Define Professional with more questions than answers about what I wanted to do, I expected my search to be different and less aggressive than many clients at the firm who were more clearly defined executives. I didn't think I would *ever* have a full-page list of target companies. Over time, I maintained a short list of around ten organizations within each search strategy I pursued.

The focus of this coaching session was preparing for a call with a recruiter from another consulting firm on my target list. I was frustrated by more questions from my coach about my ability to convince a consulting firm I could transfer capabilities from my corporate role to meet their needs. We didn't seem to have a meeting of the minds on this possibility.

For the upcoming call, I jumped on the job posting because I connected with someone in the firm through my network. If not for this posted job, I would have waited until I felt more ready to connect with this person. The firm's emphasis on associate referrals led to an initial screening call with an internal recruiter.

The recruiter asked why I was no longer in my previous job. I answered the question, but didn't take control and move the conversation to positive messages. Even though I knew exactly what I was supposed to do, I let a heavy silence fill the empty space. Clearly, I needed more practice with my Departure Statement (Activity #4).

Crisis of Confidence and Imposter Syndrome

After my first two calls to consulting firms went nowhere, I was back on my emotional roller coaster. One moment I believed in my talent and job-worthiness, and then doubted it in the next. I had many dark moments, often in or close to tears. Despite self-imposed pressure to begin networking, I wasn't confident about my readiness to contact people I knew or wanted to know. I certainly wasn't ready to interact with potential employers.

My brother-in-law advised me to find other ways to connect with people until I was ready for important job search and networking interactions. Seeming like an excellent idea, I spent time with friends and family and attended a few low-key networking events.

Clashing with my coach about search strategies and losing the battle to define myself professionally caused a head-on collision with the imposter syndrome. Self-doubt led me to question the veracity of my past contributions and capabilities. Were my accomplishments real, or was I faking it?

Before my next coaching session, I emailed a description of the consulting firm role I envisioned and planned to reality test. We had no further communication before my next appointment, which was unusual. I wasn't sure if this change in our pattern was due to schedule conflicts or our apparent impasse about my search. Around this time, several close friends and family members asked if I was still getting what I needed from coaching. Despite my frustrations, I was determined to get as much value as I could from the outplacement process. I was not ready to walk away.

One Thing Leads to Another

Believing my documents were in good shape, I identified seven people in management consulting to reality test my ideas with. I planned to approach each person through LinkedIn, email, phone, and, maybe, face-to-face meetings.

I was still following the suggestion to start with less-critical connections and save the most important for later, when I would be more articulate.

Favorable responses from people on my consulting list resulted in two calls and a lunch meeting. To make these conversations easy for my contacts and fruitful for me, I decided what to send each person in advance. I hoped these exploratory conversations would provide important insights about the viability of my primary search objective.

When networking is done well, many people go out of their way to help you connect with others they think might be helpful. The person I would meet for lunch the following week was actively thinking about others in the consulting arena he might help me connect with. Another former colleague introduced me to one of his connections on LinkedIn. The process was much like following clues in a scavenger hunt. I expected a series of connections to emerge this way in the next phase of my transition.

 **Insights: Face-to-Face Meetings
The Holy Grail of Networking?**

Consistent with considering myself an introvert, my preferred communication steps follow this sequence when I want to connect with someone new:

1. Send a personalized invitation to connect on LinkedIn; request the person's email address if it's not listed

2. Correspond through email

3. Request and conduct a phone call

4. Request a face-to-face meeting—maybe

I was often told that in-person meetings were the only type worth having. For those who believe it's the only way to truly connect and achieve their networking goals, it's a waste of time to interact any other way. But asking for a "Holy Grail" face-to-face meeting was one of the hardest things for me throughout my search.

I've experienced the advantages of face-to-face interactions in networking and work situations. Collaborating at work can be easier and more productive once you've met someone in person. But, done well, interacting through LinkedIn, email, phone, or videoconferences is also productive.

During my transition, more people responded to LinkedIn invitations and emails when I requested a call rather than a meeting. This made total sense based on how busy most people were, and how prevalent and engaging electronic and remote communications had become. Of course, I don't know what else might have happened had I stretched beyond my social comfort zone to meet more people in person.

However, as digital natives rule the world, the power of electronic communications is exploding. The supremacy of traditional, face-to-face meetings is declining as online collaboration and social media platforms proliferate. While completing this book, people were recruiting, applying for jobs, and collaborating on social media platforms I had never heard of.

The Search Continues Until Holiday Break

Between November and December, there were fewer than four weeks before business would wind down. I wanted to reach mid-December feeling satisfied with the connections I had made so far. I also heeded suggestions to end mid-December with a few appointments scheduled for early January.

Networking kicked in to high gear for a month before the holidays. My job search became my primary focus and writing took a backseat. Actually, it was thrown out of the car.

I was pleased with the activity I generated through applications and networking in my management consulting search strategy. I also experienced a common phenomenon among people in transition—getting valuable help from people I didn't expect, and disappointingly less value from some I expected to get it from. Surprisingly fruitful interactions took place with people I almost didn't bother to meet with.

With mid-December upon us, I took a two-week vacation that was planned before I lost my job. I left home with a strong sense of satisfaction about what I had accomplished in three months. I was comfortable with where I was leaving my search and how I would be ready to pick it back up in January.

It was often challenging to reenter work after vacations, sometimes even after weekends. My plan was to return from vacation January 2 and give myself and everybody else most of the following week to get back in action after the holidays.

Months 4 to 7: Trial and Error
Job Searching and Networking
Full Speed Ahead ... No Writing

*Success consists of going from
failure to failure without
loss of enthusiasm.*
— WINSTON CHURCHILL

As planned, I eased back into job searching and networking in the second and third weeks of January, and resumed weekly coaching sessions. Besides getting dressed and out of the house, meetings with my coach provided beneficial structure, guidance, and cheerleading. Networking meetings became more fruitful and enjoyable than I expected.

Applying online for every opportunity of interest generated a satisfactory number of interviews. Some weeks were sparse; others quite active. Once I found jobs that interested me, writing cover letters to position myself as a strong fit was important and time consuming.

As in previous searches, my pile of applications grew and evolved in different directions. Rejections and non-responses were all part of the game, some more disappointing than others. Keeping a full pipeline of applications and networking activities helped me maintain resilience. You can't win if you don't take the shot!

I continued endless revisions of my résumé and LinkedIn profile as I found better ways to say things. While most people urged me to stop making changes, I became more comfortable with this being an ongoing part of my process. My writing hiatus continued during these four months when my search momentum was strong.

Four Search Strategies

While navigating many ups and downs, I pursued four search strategies in months four through eighteen. It's common to pursue more than one direction at a time—particularly if you are a Hard-to-Define Professional or not sure what you want to do next.

My emphasis varied while I worked on three concurrent strategies. Strategy #1 began with a wide funnel that I narrowed and focused as I progressed through four strategies over time. The first three strategies that follow describe: target companies; ideal roles; search and networking goals and activities; challenges; and outcomes. They demonstrate how I uncovered and pursued jobs that were not typical, clearly defined roles. In the end, I shifted to focus exclusively on Strategy #4. All of these strategies demonstrate Inventive Career Transitions (PART III) and my Sweet Spot Job Search Method (PART IV) in action.

Fashionistas might compare my job search approach to shopping at T.J.Maxx® and Marshalls®. If you don't know what you're looking for, and you can fit into different sizes, you have to comb through many racks of clothing in several sizes. Shopping this way, we find buried treasures, but only by digging through racks and racks of clothes we don't even consider trying on.

Men are more likely to relate to aimlessly wandering the aisles at The Home Depot®, Lowe's®, Costco®, or Sam's Club®. You might go there to buy one thing and come out with a full shopping cart.

Time consuming? Yep. But it's a great analogy for a Sweet Spot Job Search. You might think I'm strange, but I enjoy hunting for buried treasures. I *like* finding and applying for rare, sweet spot jobs that fit my capabilities and interests, and then waiting to see if I get a response.

When I'm in search mode, I enjoy the daily habit of wading through job postings—hunting and gathering for hidden treasures—just like shopping. Even after I land a job, I continue receiving a few daily alerts. This lets me keep my finger on the pulse of how the job search process is evolving, particularly in my areas of interest and geographic market.

Search Strategy #1:
Assorted Corporate and Nonprofit Roles

This catchall search strategy was an example of casting a wide net to uncover hidden treasures—a variety of unusual jobs I *could* and *wanted* to do. I used this method to land all of my previous jobs.

In this search, exploring a broad array of organizations and roles provided information about my local job market and helped me position myself for attractive opportunities.

If you've been out of the job market for several years, are not sure what you want to do, or are considering a career change, this kind of exploration is invaluable—especially early in your search. It's a great way to discover different types of jobs that do and don't interest you.

Target Companies

Finding jobs through this search strategy was more about the nature of the work than creating a list of target companies. I considered a wide variety of organizations that offered products and services I would feel good about being associated with.

The ideal organization would have a purpose or mission I cared about, work I *could* and *wanted* to do, and people I enjoyed working with. I thought I could add the most value in service and nonprofit sectors. Jobs I applied for were in several types of organizations:

- Healthcare-related services
- Nonprofits
- Nonprofit/Association management services
- Executive education
- Higher education

Ideal Role

I looked for roles related to communications, member services, nontechnical project management, and program management.

Search and Networking Goals

This multifaceted direction required me to cast a super-wide net to find hidden treasures—unusual roles that could be buried among thousands of posted jobs, and listed with an infinite variety of titles.

Search and Networking Activities

I set up a wide variety of keyword searches and daily alerts on several job sites and skimmed hundreds of job postings each day. Keywords in the *job title* field included project manager, program manager, client relationship, and coordinator. I also set up search alerts on several nonprofit job sites.

As for networking, I was introduced and connected with people in numerous organizations. While many interactions were informative and enjoyable, none led to job offers.

Challenges

This job search method takes time, patience, and daily discipline. I spent several hours, seven days a week, pouring through hundreds of positions from several job boards, applying as soon as possible for each job of interest. Often finding more sweet spot jobs on Fridays and Saturdays, my desire to be among the first applicants meant working on applications during the weekend.

Applying for these jobs involved any combination of an online application, a résumé, and a customized cover letter and/or email. Writing strong cover letters carefully tailored for each job was the most time-consuming element. Completing the total package for each job could take two to three hours.

Outcomes

I applied, connected on LinkedIn, and had numerous phone interviews for interesting roles in many organizations. Over time, I uncovered reasons why most of the positions weren't right for me (high pressure, long hours, low pay).

This exploration confirmed I would be selective about the work I wanted to do and where I wanted to do it. Although it didn't result in a job this time, the research helped me develop my approach to opportunities within my other search strategies.

Search Strategy #2:
Internal Services Role in a Management Consulting Firm

Target Companies

This was my priority search strategy. I was most interested in landing an internal services role in a small- to mid-size consulting firm, ranging in size from 20 to 200 people. The ideal firm would be purpose-driven, with strong thought leadership and intellectual property I found compelling. Areas of interest included leadership, strategic alignment, corporate culture, employee and customer engagement, collaboration, and learning.

Ideal Role

My target role involved collaborating with consultants and subject matter experts to design, market, and deliver products and services to clients. I envisioned helping consultants plan and manage client engagements, and writing and editing a range of content—marketing materials, articles, web content, client proposals, and presentations.

Rather than being a consultant, these internal functions would be akin to behind-the-scenes roles I was used to playing. I've always been content as the woman behind the curtain, not out in front. Another reason I didn't want to be a consultant was because I didn't want to live out of a suitcase with frequent travel to client locations.

Search and Networking Goals

My objective was to land a job that existed or, highly unlikely, have one created for me. I aimed to:

- Reality test the feasibility of the role I envisioned by speaking with consultants I had worked with and others they might introduce me to

- Gather input to clearly define the ideal role and hone my ability to explain it in conversations

- Position my experience and capabilities to fit and add value in the role and generate responses to online applications

- Connect with people who might help me land a job that fit my criteria

Search and Networking Activities

Despite being most interested in this direction, it was not where I was spending most of my time and energy. When a friend asked where I was focusing my efforts in relation to what I wanted to accomplish, the conversation caused me to redirect my activity toward this strategy.

In my last role, I collaborated with more than ten consulting firms on initiatives related to leadership, strategic planning, and employee engagement. Connections in these firms became critical to my search strategy. Interactions with a wide range of consultants included sole practitioners; principals in small firms; and current and former partners in three of the "Big 4" accounting and consulting firms: Deloitte, EY (formerly Ernst & Young, and PwC (PricewaterhouseCoopers).

Conversations focused on specific jobs I applied for, information gathering, and requests for introductions. Combined with keywords and phrases from job postings, these interactions helped me develop my story and a targeted résumé that described the role I was seeking, how my experience related to the role, and how I could add value.

Besides management consulting targets, I explored and generated good traction in the corporate training segment of consulting. This direction was somewhat related to the firms and roles I was targeting, but not quite a bullseye. Even though I'm not an instructional designer, I had more interviews and got closer to offers than I expected. Once I concluded this niche was not in my sweet spot, I discontinued a few conversations that could have gone further.

Challenges

It took a while to clearly distinguish the internal services roles I was seeking from being a consultant. Some people couldn't understand the difference. Rather than the internal staff role I envisioned, my coach seemed to zero in on my wanting to be a consultant.

From the marketplace perspective, larger firms were biased toward hiring MBAs from top business schools and experienced people from other consulting firms, especially the "Big 4."

Networking and reality testing illuminated the common "eat what you kill" business model in consulting firms. As in many professional service firms, compensation and advancement depend heavily on how much revenue you generate through business development (sales) and billable time. And, like most industries, consulting firms are under intense pressure to run lean. This leaves them hesitant to add staff (overhead) that doesn't directly generate revenue.

From the perspective of my background, I needed to create a résumé that described 20 years of experience in one company as a convincing fit for the consulting firm role I was seeking. My approach was to describe many aspects of my previous role as internal consulting, and emphasize the consulting firms and engagements I had been involved with.

As with my previous career changes, people were skeptical about how realistic it was for me to transition from a corporate environment to a consulting firm role. Staying the course to switch industries absolutely requires extra perseverance and resilience.

Outcomes
The management consulting firm direction did not come to fruition during the first seven months of my search. Despite promising traction from online applications and robust networking, it didn't happen.

⊘ **TIP: Dedicate the most effort to your priority career direction(s).** It seems obvious to devote the most time and energy to pursuing your top priority. However, if your priority is a new direction, you might feel intimidated and resist contacting people who can best help you. It's essential to work through anxiety or lack of confidence that might cause you to hesitate to do the most important things you need to do. Even if it doesn't pan out, you'll know you gave it your best shot.

Hitting a Wall with My Search and My Coach

Coming to the end of the road with several promising consulting firm opportunities, my hopes for this strategy faded. I had been working seven days a week at an overdrive level of intensity. Even though I enjoyed networking more than I expected, sustaining momentum for many months had taken its toll.

After seven months on my roller coaster ride of intensive soul searching, job searching, and networking, I hit a wall with burnout, exhaustion, and depression. I even cried a few times when I talked to people at networking meetings. I could no longer stir up the energy to meet with individuals, attend career transition events, or have in-person sessions with my coach.

Due to my coach's tight schedule and my state of mind, we conducted three appointments by phone, then I stopped scheduling sessions. My coach sent several emails urging me to sustain the intensity of my search full speed ahead, especially through June, before recruiting and networking would slow down for the summer (another common myth).

While not explicitly discussing with my coach how fragile I had become, I was depressed and could not continue networking. In the shape I was in, it wasn't productive to keep pushing myself out there to talk to people.

With distance, I thought about why I had become frustrated with my outplacement process. My coach did a great job guiding me through tactical assignments. But we seemed to miss the forest through the trees by not clearly defining several search strategies earlier in my process. We didn't seem to be in sync about my interests and aspirations, or the situations I wanted to avoid.

Depression and anxiety set in when things were out of my control, especially while waiting to hear about next steps on applications or interviews. My inability to concentrate even prevented me from enjoying reading—normally a favorite activity.

Knowing I would not get through this alone, with a nudge from my husband, I started therapy. In addition to weekly sessions, my therapist referred me to a psychiatrist who prescribed medication for depression and anxiety.

> ✅ **TIP: Take care of your mental health.** Seek professional help if you feel depressed and/or anxious. Psychological or medical attention is essential if you feel helpless or hopeless about the future, or have any suicidal thoughts.

Months 8 to 10: Disruption
Better Living Through Chemistry

My roller coaster ride continued in months eight through ten. Still emotionally raw, I alternated between feeling like I had been hit by a gigantic tidal wave and riding a gentle ocean current of small ups and downs I could handle with ease. When my search went well, I felt optimistic. During low points, especially when opportunities fell through, I fell apart.

Liz Ryan, founder of www.humanworkplace.com, published a compelling blog post called "How to Get Your Mojo Back"—a perfect description of how I felt when I crashed and lost all belief in the value I could bring to a new job. This blog post resonated deeply because my mojo had slipped so far from my grasp and I was struggling to recapture any sign of resilience (https://www.linkedin.com/pulse/20140722005130-52594-how-to-get-your-mojo-back).

If you've been depressed, you know how hard it is to get yourself to do anything when nothing makes you smile—including things you usually enjoy. How I dealt with free time was always an accurate gauge of my emotional wellbeing. When depressed, I lost interest in everything, time moved slowly, and sleep became a frequent escape route. With limited interests or hobbies, I felt anxious when my husband asked, "Retire and do what?" In contrast, when feeling content and at my best, there wasn't enough time to do everything I wanted to do.

Here I was, right in the middle of a battle between depression and resilience. Depression was winning. As my prescriptions took effect, depression and anxiety subsided gradually, and I tried to do things that made me feel happier.

Changing Directions

Once the consulting firm strategy dissolved, I knew I needed help to shift directions. Despite major challenges, I decided to try to land a role similar to the job I lost by searching in a wide variety of organizations. With assistance from the president of my outplacement firm, I redirected my search toward a third search strategy—chief of staff and special assistant to CEO roles. He helped reposition my résumé from consulting firm roles to this direction.

Search Strategy #3:
Chief of Staff and Special Assistant to CEO

Target Companies
If they exist, positions like the one I had are unique to each company. It would be hard to find a sweet spot role that combined work I *could* and *wanted* to do, leaders I wanted to work with, and a place I wanted to work.

Without a definitive target list, I still focused on service, nonprofit, and academic organizations. Consistent with my prior experience and beliefs about where I could thrive, I shied away from global, public, and manufacturing companies. Many people thought I was misdirected in limiting my options this way.

Ideal Role
The most attractive roles had a special assistant title. There were few, but I was excited when I found them. For those advertised as executive assistant, I applied when enough of the work seemed to be at a higher level than typical administrative duties.

I believed it was possible to find a high-level staff role that would leverage my transferable skills. Like Goldilocks, I tried to find a job that was not too administrative on the left; not too strategic on the right; but "just right" in the middle of a continuum. On the administrative end, I did not want to be glued to my computer managing the details of my boss's calendar. On the strategic end, I did not have experience in areas such as mergers and acquisitions, setting up new lines of business, and financial analysis.

Like my previous job, my sweet spot role in the middle would include collaborating with executives and consultants to manage strategic planning activities; writing and editing; nontechnical project and program management; managing stakeholder relationships; and planning, facilitating, and documenting workshops and meetings.

Search and Networking Goals
Well aware of the challenges, I set out to combine intensive online searches and networking. There were three possible avenues to succeed with this strategy:

1. **Find and land a needle-in-the-haystack job advertised online.** These jobs *are* posted, but they are rare. I believed this was the most likely scenario. Others viewed it as impossible and believed goals #2 and #3 below were more likely.

2. **Network to land a sweet spot job that would never be advertised.** Although less likely than goal #1 above, I viewed this scenario as somewhat possible.

3. **Network to have a job created for me because my new boss would realize what I could do for him or her.** Quite a few career coaches and people I networked with believed this happened a lot. I viewed it as rare and improbable.

Search and Networking Activities
Résumé. Using keywords and phrases from job postings that matched what I was looking for, I repositioned my internal

consulting-oriented experience and capabilities to fit this direction. This was the easiest résumé to create because the target role was closest to my last position.

Online searches. I set up keyword searches and daily alerts to find and apply for jobs that seemed like a good fit. These activities are described fully in the 25 Activities section:

- Captured as many opportunities as possible by casting a wide net of keyword searches in job titles (e.g., chief of staff, special assistant, executive coordinator, executive assistant)

- Submitted applications and/or résumés and cover letters as soon as possible after jobs were posted

- Addressed letters to specific people when I could identify hiring managers (potential bosses) or the correct HR/recruiting contacts

Networking. Doubting either would happen, I networked to find or have someone create a chief of staff or special assistant job that would never be advertised.

Once I reached certain milestones, my outplacement firm provided the opportunity to meet with four of their principals. The objectives were to practice networking conversations, get feedback and ideas about search strategies, and identify introductions and connections the principals might provide. This was one of the most valuable parts of my outplacement process.

Before and after I stopped meeting with my coach, these conversations led to phone and/or in-person meetings with approximately 20 people. Most introductions required me to draft an email about myself for the principal to use, with proactive follow-up by me. With a full pipeline of new contacts, I paced myself during the next several months to do as much networking as I could handle.

Late in my search, I used LinkedIn to find local people with current or previous chief of staff titles. I contacted people whose past or present roles were close to what I envisioned for myself. My steps were to invite them to connect on LinkedIn, send an email if I could get their direct email address, schedule a call, and, if I could find the courage, request a face-to-face meeting. I connected with six or seven people to learn about their chief of staff roles. None of the interactions led to specific interviews or offers, but several became important people in my network.

Challenges
As mentioned, these positions are hard to find and land for several reasons:

- If the role exists, only one chief of staff or special assistant reports to the top person, and a few others might report to other senior executives.

- These positions can be hard to land from outside the company and the industry.

- Some companies use these roles as rotational training grounds for new MBAs or high-potential leaders.

Amplifying the obstacles for finding and landing these elusive jobs, some people could not grasp the difference between a special assistant and an executive assistant. I was shocked by how many job postings included both administrative and strategic work. Companies were looking for über executive assistants who could do all the traditional administrative tasks plus much of the higher-level work I did in my prior role. I thought companies were misguided in thinking the same person could or would want to perform this range of responsibilities.

In my experience, few executive assistants were prepared to be strategic or conceptual thought partners to executives. Nor did I know many (any?) people with strong business acumen who wanted to perform routine, labor-intensive administrative tasks. This challenge led me to a major mistake and meltdown in Month 11.

Outcomes

I applied for all chief of staff and special assistant to CEO jobs of interest, plus executive assistant jobs in which higher-level work seemed to far exceed administrative tasks. Many online applications resulted in phone and face-to-face interviews. Some conversations were mutually curtailed when it became evident that a job was too administrative for my skills and interests.

Three particularly exciting opportunities are described below. After applying online, leveraging connections and introductions might have contributed to getting as far as I did with two of them, but none generated offers.

1. **Special assistant to the CEO at a leading children's hospital.** After a personal introduction to a senior HR executive and several in-depth phone conversations, I did not progress to face-to-face interviews. It seemed unlikely to land this high-profile role because I did not have healthcare experience.

2. **Special assistant to the dean of a prestigious school within a top Ivy League university.** After a phone screen, I was invited to a face-to-face interview. I might have gotten this far because I contacted a former coworker who worked there and sent an email about me to the dean. The role seemed like a great fit. It also seemed unlikely to land this high-profile role without university experience, and I was pretty sure they intended to fill the job internally.

3. **Executive assistant to the CEO at a boutique financial services company.** This role supported an executive I thought would be great to work with in a company that interested me. After one phone interview and three face-to-face interviews, I met with the founder and CEO. He concluded I would be bored and dissatisfied in the role because it was too administrative.

   The CEO also told me he had just hired someone for the higher-level role I was seeking. Having worked on some projects with the person he hired, he said he would not have known how, nor would he have tried, to advertise that position. This confirmed the hard truth that the position I wanted would be hard (but *not* impossible) to land by applying online.

⊘ **TIP: Make it easy for people to introduce you to people in their network.** When people offer to introduce you to people they know, offer to draft an email they can edit and send to each person. Develop core boilerplate copy, and customize additional material for each situation. It's important to be proactive and timely with your follow-through on all introductions offered and accepted.

🗸 **TIP: Keep filling your pipeline with new possibilities.** Like any sales process, a full pipeline can keep you productive and prevent meltdowns when doors close on opportunities you were excited about. Using a Network Tracking Report to manage my pipeline was one of the most helpful tools in my search (Activity 14: Network Tracking Report).

Month 11: Crash Landing
False Positive and Falling Apart

False Positive

After applying online and completing several interviews, I was thrilled to accept a position as special assistant to the head of a prestigious preparatory school near Philadelphia. I looked forward to working in a non-corporate environment, collaborating with a great leader, and being involved in purposeful and interesting work to help students become future leaders.

Against all odds, I landed this job as one of more than 465 applicants—with no connections or introductions at the school. The HR manager commented on how impressive my résumé was and said I kept rising to the top of the candidate pool. So, yes, you *can* land jobs by responding to online job postings— even without connections in the organizations.

In every conversation, up to and including the offer, people emphasized that the head of the school was looking for someone who would be "more" and "different" from a typical executive assistant. My ability to be a significant contributor to higher-level strategic work with the school's leadership team and long-range plans was a major factor in being selected. My new boss and I were excited about the instant, strong rapport we felt and looked forward to working together.

Believing the role was a great fit with the senior staff role I was looking for, and that it would provide attractive work-life balance, I accepted the job at less than half of my previous compensation. They agreed to change my title from executive assistant to special assistant. I anticipated a challenging and fulfilling experience as both thought partner and assistant to the leader of the school.

Starting the job in early August, I expected to ease into my new role with lighter summer hours (9:00 a.m. to 3:00 p.m.). In reality, 10-hour days and work that would never be done caused immediate concerns. It seemed like I, and everyone involved in hiring me, had minimized the fact that the largest portion of the job was an immense and intense executive assistant role. In many ways, changing the title from executive assistant to special assistant was cosmetic.

The impressive top executive required an exceptionally skilled assistant to manage a demanding and ever-changing calendar. This involved scheduling many complex meetings with faculty, administrators, and extremely busy board members and parents. Every time I turned around, a complicated meeting, or a new evening or weekend event was added to the calendar or had to be scheduled. Added to this were general administrative duties (communications, travel arrangements, expense reports); state recordkeeping (manually counting the number of school days for each grade level); traditional rituals (gatherings with the head of the school); and major events (graduation).

Another significant part of the job was collaborating with the new secretary of the board of trustees to complete time-consuming administrative tasks. Adding to this workload, the head of the school and new chairman of the board were embarking on a multi-year process to significantly enhance communications and procedures for the board and its growing list of committees. Combining routine board administration with the desired improvements expanded this significant aspect of the job.

The role seemed to encompass two or three jobs rolled into one. Even if one person *could* do the combined jobs, I couldn't imagine anyone who would *want* to. With the heavy administrative workload, I couldn't envision there being much (if any) room for more interesting and challenging work that had been so attractive to everyone involved in the hiring process. I couldn't see this job *ever* becoming a manageable and enjoyable situation. Work-life balance did not seem remotely possible.

Struggling through each day, I tried to remember the *normal* learning curve for any new job. I also understood the *extensive* learning curve I would have in the academic environment that was new for me. In several meetings with my boss and the HR leaders, they tried to convince me that everything would be fine once I got through the first board meeting, and then the first academic year. About seven weeks away from the first board meeting, I was afraid I would land in the hospital before it took place.

I experienced a level of anxiety I had never felt before. Several evenings I came home and fell apart—crying, rocking back and forth, and wringing my hands. I was too anxious to eat during the day, my GI system stopped working right, I had dry mouth, and I couldn't sleep. Frequent sensations of "elevator stomach" felt like my insides were dropping on an amusement park ride. Friends and family were concerned.

The last person to leave at around 6:00 each evening, I asked myself what I was doing in this job at this stage of my life. I am *not* a quitter, but I would not survive this level of anxiety, particularly after what I had been through in the past 11 months.

So, my eighth day on the job was my last day on the job. I had almost quit a few days earlier but agreed to stay and try to make it work. In the end, it wasn't the sweet spot job I was looking for and it wasn't meant to be. I made the profoundly difficult and absolutely necessary decision to walk away.

Although I felt terrible about leaving the school in this situation, it had to be done. People at the school, family, and friends commended my courage to walk away so quickly.

Better Living through More Chemistry

Leaving the job at the school brought on my most severe meltdown of depression and anxiety. Three search directions had dissolved before my eyes. With no ideas about what kind of work I *could* or *wanted* to do, I was afraid I might never work again. I felt totally lost, and panic set in about what to do next.

On top of leaving the job, this crash landing was exacerbated by a significant financial loss. I became ineligible for up to $10,000 in unemployment compensation because I walked away from what the state considered "suitable work." Fortunately, I didn't also lose my COBRA health coverage. Devastation had kept me from being my normal, efficient self who would have canceled my policy as soon as I started the new job.

Characterizing this experience as a false positive, it felt like a huge failure and caused me to lose interest and confidence in all career directions I had pursued. Talk about losing my mojo! My physical anxiety symptoms persisted and got worse. Everything—large and small—I needed to think about or do made me anxious, and I had constant elevator-stomach sensations.

It was fortunate that I had already started therapy and prescriptions for depression and anxiety. But I knew I needed additional help to get through this rock-bottom situation. While adjusting to an additional prescription I was in bad shape, alternating between intense anxiety and numbing depression.

Even while treading water, waiting for my anxiety and depression to recede, I felt pressure to resume my job search. I went through the motions of looking through daily job alerts but didn't find roles I wanted to pursue. Surprised by how many executive assistant "plus" roles were posted, I kept wondering who *could* or would *want* to do everything they were looking for in one person. I found no chief of staff or special assistant to CEO jobs to apply for.

 Insights: The Broken Interview Process Means Yes and No Are Not Forever

My false positive was an unfortunate mismatch that gave me new insights about why so many new hires (over 40%) don't succeed in their new jobs beyond 18-24 months. I've also heard that 80% of employee turnover is due to bad hiring decisions.

These scenarios mean that neither "Yes" or "No" answers are necessarily long-term results. If you were the second or third choice and the person hired washes out, you have a good chance to be number one in the next round. After I left the school, they probably contacted their second or third top candidate to fill the job I vacated. I bet that person was surprised to receive that call!

In my situation, mutual interviewing and due diligence seemed to result in distorted views about the job being a good fit. In retrospect, I think we got excited by our perceptions, but didn't do enough thorough exploration to ensure we all got what we were looking for.

Given the big career shift for me, I wish they had further explained the details in the job description and how I would be spending my time. I wish I had asked more questions and shadowed my predecessor before accepting the position. Had I understood more about the true nature of the job, I would not have accepted it.

As I gained distance from this false positive, I concluded there were many great things about the job, but there was much more wrong than right for me. After I fell apart and recovered, many insights helped me move forward to a much better place.

☑️ **TIP: Make job interviews a two-way process.** Many HR professionals, recruiters, and hiring managers need training and better processes for skillful interviewing. As a job seeker, you own at least half of the responsibility to ensure a great fit. Use books, online information, and local resources to learn as much as you can about interviewing, including how to answer common and difficult questions.

Other key activities include learning about the company, speaking with current or past employees, and preparing thoughtful questions. Don't be afraid to ask questions and walk away if it's not a good fit—sooner is better than later!

✅ TIP: Wait six months to broadcast your new job. Don't be too quick to update your LinkedIn profile and notify your network about your safe landing. I wish I had heard this before I emailed more than 30 people about the exciting new job I left after eight days.

Month 12: Epiphany
Working With Words!

This Book is Born

Fortunately, with the benefit of therapy and prescriptions, my anxiety leveled out to a more comfortable place after about three weeks. As I was ready, I took baby steps to put myself back together, but I had no idea what that would look like.

Pushing through hesitation, I registered for a community night school class about writing your first book. The course focused on developing a strong book outline and provided information about self-publishing. I was excited about moving forward to expand my journal into a book, yet doubtful about my ability to publish it.

Around the same time, a former colleague recommended *The War of Art* by Steven Pressfield because it had inspired her to write. I read the book the following weekend and returned to working on my book Monday. The book provided powerful insights about moving from resistance and procrastination to "doing the work" of writing. I was inspired by Pressfield's notion that the more afraid artists are about doing a piece of work, the more sure we can be that we must do it. Rather than limited to artists, this probably applies to anybody afraid to tackle anything big they want to do in their lives.

Feeling both compelled and anxious, I read and edited around 30 journal pages I had written but not looked at since December. I was determined to bring a complete outline of the book to the first session of my seven-week class. To my amazement, the initial structure of the whole book came together one day before the first anniversary of D-Day. Getting this done so easily seemed like a sign that this class was exactly the right thing at the right time.

I was almost ready to move beyond editing to writing new parts of my story, but not quite. My therapist observed that I might not be ready to write more because I hadn't yet written the next chapter of my life. It made complete sense that I needed to know more about my next career move before I would be ready to write new sections of my book.

First Anniversary of D-Day

In the larger scheme of war, climate change, and death of a loved one, my job loss *was* a small thing—yet parts of the experience were devastating. It had been a long year, full of extreme emotions and difficult days.

I marked the one-year anniversary by spending time with a friend, away from my office. I bought myself a small gift to commemorate my job loss and celebrate the nascent beginning of my next chapter.

I AM a Writer | Editor | Proofreader!

As I resumed working on this book, I felt more content than I had in a long time. Even more significant, a new possibility emerged and blossomed into a life-changing epiphany. I realized I was meant to work with words!

I had always enjoyed significant aspects of my jobs focused on writing and editing. I recalled my ability to interview thought leaders and subject matter experts to help them develop conceptual ideas and put them on paper. In my last job, I deepened my conviction that words matter—a lot! They have the power to create shared meaning that engages and inspires people to act, hopefully with all good intentions.

After walking away from the job at the school, I was drawn to writing and editing more than ever before, and more than anything else. In the false positive situation, I got sick from anxiety and tuned into clear signals telling me it would not work. At this stage, visceral cues drew me toward writing, editing, and proofreading jobs. This direction felt more right than any search strategy I had pursued in the past year.

⊘ **TIP: Let your instincts guide you to what you _want_ to do.** Listen, sense, and honor your inner voice and physical cues about what you _do_ and _don't_ want to do. Lean in to clues about what attracts and excites you and what makes you anxious—wanting to walk (or run) in the other direction.

Month 13: Reconstitution
Putting Myself Back Together—Fast!

_We create the opportunities
that come our way._

Search Strategy #4:
Writer | Editor | Proofreader—This is IT!

Just past the one-year mark, I had finally figured out what I *wanted* to do professionally. Moving forward with my new search strategy—writing, editing, and proofreading—I set up new keyword searches and alerts. Using a slightly revised résumé, I got immediate responses to applications for editing and proofreading contracts. It became evident right away that I was on a promising new course.

After losing my 20-year job and walking away from the school, I wanted a long-term temporary contract. I was hesitant to dive into a full-time "permanent" position—a misnomer since the Global financial crisis. One of the first staffing firm recruiters who called about a contract asked me to create a résumé that laser-focused on my writing, editing, and proofreading experience—a monumental turning point in my story.

Based on the recruiter's request, I created the third incarnation of my résumé. To recap: the first version was for the assorted variety (Search Strategy #1) and consulting firm roles (Search Strategy #2); the second was for chief of staff and special assistant to CEO roles (Search Strategy #3); and this third version was for writing, editing, and proofreading jobs (Search Strategy #4). This version featured all editorial work I had done throughout my career.

This was also the right time to refocus my LinkedIn profile for my new search strategy. I kept enough content about my C-level corporate experience and capabilities to be considered for higher-level communications jobs, and left the door open (just a crack) for chief of staff and special assistant to CEO roles. It felt like a big step, but it was necessary for my new direction.

Despite the false positive that led to my lowest point, it took less than a month to put myself back together and move forward. When that crisis left a terrifying void, things could have gone one of two ways. I could have had an extended stay in a dangerously dark place, or I could invent a new way to think about my next chapter. I'm not sure how I found resilience to do the latter, and much sooner than expected.

Entering D-Day plus 13 months (only three weeks after leaving the school job), I felt more optimistic that things would happen when they were meant to be. I was less anxious, taking things in stride, and enjoying the freedom and flexibility to do what I wanted, when I wanted. My therapist suggested I memorize how this felt in every way, and store the memory for a future setback that might leave me feeling depressed and anxious. In the meantime, knowing things *would* get better would be a life raft to hang onto.

My husband was pleased about my being more relaxed, and I was cautiously confident good things would happen. On occasion, we both worried I might not get back to working and earning enough to bridge us to the retirement lifestyle we wanted. We needed to keep checking in with each other about my direction and our finances, and make time and space to explore our goals and plans together.

The XYZ of Things: Xanax y Zentangle®

My job search was looking up, I was back to working on this book, and my mother-in-law introduced me to Zentangle®-inspired artwork. Discovering an artistic side I didn't know I had, I took this delicate pattern-drawing technique to new places with color and other embellishments. This creative endeavor had a calming effect on my anxiety by stopping irritating, repetitive thoughts in their tracks (just like Xanax). Seeking the same calming benefits, I dabbled in yoga, but only briefly. Perhaps I will revisit this in the future.

Month 14: Purpose-Driven Calling Finding Myself

To find out what one is fitted to do
and secure an opportunity to do it
is the key to happiness.
— JOHN DEWEY

I Finally Know Who I Am!

My new, laser-focused résumé rocked! Online applications generated additional responses and several interviews. My confidence grew, as did my sense of being on the verge of finding work I really wanted to do.

Because traction with this résumé was so strong, I was selective about the first contract I accepted. I walked away from several interviews and one offer involving content that didn't interest me. I decided to wait for something more appealing to come my way—ideally, purpose-driven work I would find compelling.

While pursuing temporary editing and proofreading contracts, I also positioned myself for freelance work in this direction. Despite believing I was on the cusp of something great, I was hesitant to claim victory. I had felt optimistic and confident before—but not to this degree.

She's Baaack: Sententia (My Muse) Returns!

As the belief took shape that writing and editing could become my next chapter, Sententia returned to channel her words through me. Beyond editing, I was writing new content because I had to, capturing a constant waterfall of ideas before they floated away. If you met Sententia in PART I: The Backstory, you know how she influenced this book. If you skipped that part, suffice it to say she is my Muse who inspires me to write.

In addition to the satisfaction I got from writing this book, I was cautiously convinced that writing, editing, and proofreading opportunities would continue coming my way.

I seemed to be moving toward one career scenario I had envisioned—a combination of contract and freelance work. I experimented and worked toward creating a combination of temporary contracts and freelance projects to generate enough income for this stage of our lives—and leave enough time to write this book.

And now comes the best part. As I pursued writing, editing, and proofreading opportunities, Search Strategy #4 became the triumphant next chapter of my life and work.

Months 15 to 17: Reinvention
Creating My New Career

Contract Editing and Proofreading Assignments

To provide a core of stable income, I wanted to land a full-time contract that would last between three and eighteen months. The first direction I focused on was editing and proofreading contracts in human resources, corporate communications, and marketing. When I felt comfortable with the subject matter, I also applied for jobs that involved writing original content.

Within a few weeks of submitting applications, speaking with recruiters, and interviewing for temporary assignments, I was thrilled to be selected for a full-time, three-month contract as an HR communications editor. It was in one of the nation's top financial services companies, also a leading "Best Place to Work" in my geographic region.

Despite being in financial services, it was one of the best large companies I could imagine working in. My financial services experience undoubtedly helped me land this contract (10 points for my coach). My editing and proofreading experience combined with my collaborative and process improvement orientation were also key factors in being selected.

Right before accepting this contract, I had another possibility brewing in the same company and walked away from two editing contracts in other companies that were not as interesting. During my contract, I was periodically contacted by recruiters about other editing and proofreading contracts.

There were a few feeding frenzies for contracts when multiple recruiters found my résumé on CareerBuilder or Monster. Several were far from my areas of expertise (e.g., FDA submissions for pharmaceutical companies), so I would not have accepted them. These were examples of recruiters not doing their jobs to match candidates with job requirements.

I thoroughly enjoyed the three-month contract I accepted, and felt fortunate to work in one of the largest and best-managed financial services companies in the United States. I learned a lot, sharpened my editing skills, and added a few important people to my network. The company offered to extend my three-month contract for at least nine months.

During my contract, I received an alert for a job that was a 100% match for the special assistant to CEO role I had been seeking. After thinking long and hard about applying, and tuning in to my inner cues, I concluded I had no interest in going there. This decision confirmed that writing and editing was absolutely the track I wanted to be on. Success in this first three-month editing contract solidified confidence in my skills and ability to land future contracts whenever the first one ended.

Freelance Writing, Editing, Proofreading Projects

The second direction I explored included a variety of freelance work I could do from home. Each required testing to be accepted as a freelancer:

- I was a top candidate (but not selected) to edit articles for a business writer. This person found me through my LinkedIn profile.

- I was accepted as a résumé writer for an online service that paid $20 per résumé. This compensation was not commensurate with my views on the expertise and time required to create a great résumé.

- I did website testing, which paid $10 for 10-20 minutes of work. This was interesting and rewarding, but it was impossible to generate significant revenue by qualifying for sporadic tests.

- I proofread marketing research transcripts, which paid $10 for 1-3 hours of work. This was more interesting, but I was not willing to work for $3.33 per hour!

While none of these freelance work-at-home gigs took flight, I remained confident that great opportunities would come to fruition.

Freelance Job Search Coaching and Résumé Services

I have helped countless friends and family members with their résumés during the past 30 years. In this job search, after wrestling with endless opinions, researching best practices, and making hundreds of revisions, I created two of my own résumés that defied gravity. They repeatedly did their job to land in the "Yes" pile for interviews (Samples 2-A, 2-B).

When I attended career transition and networking meetings, other job seekers were fascinated by all I had learned about LinkedIn, and the success I had when applying for jobs online. This led me to offer freelance job search coaching and résumé services.

My husband and I attended a monthly career transition meeting featuring a presentation on networking. The presenter was a woman I had met through networking and stayed in touch with. To demonstrate one of her key points, she asked me to introduce myself to the room of more than 130 people. Of course, I wanted to crawl under the table.

What I stood up and said made this meeting a life-changing event: "I am a communications professional and I help people perfect their words." At the end of the meeting, we were supposed to stay and network—I wanted to leave. While my husband badgered me to stay, two women sought me out to tell me they liked what I said, and asked if I helped people with résumés. I ended up assisting both of them.

Leaving this meeting, I knew I was onto something that resonated with people. I played with different versions of "helping people perfect their words" and created a website. Within two weeks after the meeting, I had a basic website (www.WordsPerfected. net) and new business cards. I evolved my value proposition into perfecting content others have drafted or envisioned, and helping people figure out what they want to do, and then make it happen.

Rather than expecting people to find my website through keyword searches, I planned to direct potential clients there to learn more about how I could help them. It worked like a charm when people found me on LinkedIn and through referrals. Attracting as many or as few clients as I wanted, I found great satisfaction in helping people explore career options, build confidence, and create résumés and LinkedIn profiles to achieve their goals.

Author

While pursuing temporary contracts and freelance projects, I continued working toward publishing this book. My evening class provided a wealth of information about the world of self-publishing that is evolving with lightning speed. I started the class wondering how I would ever publish a book through traditional channels, and ended it knowing I would most likely self-publish.

My editing contract limited me to working 37.5 hours per week. This was a great opportunity to learn how to stop working when there was still more to be done. The work was interesting and challenging, with plenty of brain space left to write during weekends and other free time. This book became a manifestation of my combined passion for writing and editing, and helping people navigate career transitions.

Month 18: Triumph
Coming Full Circle

Business Writer and Editor in a Management Consulting Firm

While seeking contracts that resulted in my three-month editing assignment, I did not actively pursue permanent jobs. After a few days of vacillating, I pushed myself to apply online for a full-time business writer position. It was in one of the first management consulting firms I had targeted—the one in which I had my first phone conversation that went nowhere. This job didn't fit my contract and freelance goals, but I was fascinated by the company's work, and my new résumé worked its magic!

Several weeks before my editing contract started, I had several calls and interviews with the consulting firm. Trying to fill this position for more than a year, they had not found other writers with the C-level and business experience I could bring to the table. Because of their unusually long hiring process, we agreed to continue conversations while I worked in my contract position.

The week before my contract started, I completed a significant freelance writing project for the consulting company. I also completed an online course and a three-day program to gain exposure to the company's proprietary methods. In both programs, I focused on publishing this book as the challenging goal I wanted to achieve.

Both learning experiences clarified the steps I would take to publish, and gave me insights about how my perfectionism was getting in my way. These insights helped me separate my freedom to write from my obsession to edit. Many authors talk about the importance of this distinction, and it helped me make great strides toward publishing.

During my editing contract, I continued conversations with the consulting company about the writing position and worked on this book during weekends. I was poised to come full circle to land an internal services role in a consulting company that had been on my initial target list. It was an extraordinary match with the type of organization I wanted to join. The company's purpose-driven thought leadership, research, and methods transform individuals, teams, and organizations to achieve extraordinary results.

As I was writing the last sections of this book, the consulting firm offered a contract-to-hire position. I had the choice to stay in my editing contract for the rest of the year (maybe longer), or accept the business writer position in the consulting firm. Continuing the contract was attractive. Becoming a writer at this consulting firm was irresistible. I accepted the offer.

I became a full-time employee after working as a contractor for two months. Landing this position was a remarkable triumph. It was a more focused role than I envisioned when pursuing Search Strategy #2, but I had not yet zeroed in on writing and editing as the focal point of my next chapter. Eighteen months into my new job, the company felt like the place I was meant to be and I was proud of all I had done to get myself there. The opportunity to experience and write about the company's profound work was miraculous.

Happy to Stay; Always Ready to Market "Me, Inc."

Extensive due diligence, combined with the try-before-you-buy approach, increased the likelihood of a great fit for all of us. If it had turned out to not be the match we anticipated, I was confident I could land a different contract or permanent position and continue to build my freelance business.

As required by my new employer, I put my freelance business on pause, but I was excited to have it waiting in the wings for the future. Through my LinkedIn profile and networking connections I received ongoing inquiries about my availability, referred business to others, and provided limited job search coaching and résumé assistance on a pro-bono or trade-for-services basis. And, just in case I needed to make another change, I remained prepared to re-enter the job market.

I Got My Mojo Back!

Looking back on my turbulent transformation, I had mourned, recovered, discovered, and triumphed after a profound loss that shook me to my core. After losing my mojo for an extended period, I got it back by sustaining determination through wins and losses. Three hard-won victories brought back my confidence and solidified my professional reinvention:

1. Providing job search coaching and résumé services that helped other people find their way was fulfilling.

2. Sharpening my skills and contributing other value during my editing contract was exhilarating.

3. Landing my job as a business writer and editor was a remarkable triumph.

During a family gathering at a restaurant, I saw the person who had been the head of HR and handed me my walking papers on D-Day. A sure sign of my strong recovery was my ability to greet him warmly, with no hard feelings about that fateful day when he was just doing his job. I subsequently invited him to connect on LinkedIn and made light of being far from my best self *that day* in his office.

Solve No Problem Before Its Time

Traveling through this transformational tunnel was one of the most difficult times in my life. Once on the other side, I understood how *all* of it helped me find myself and work that would make me happy.

Ironically, the business writer and editor position I accepted was originally posted as the copywriter job I applied for in the second month of my transition. But I would not have been ready had I landed the job at the beginning of my search. Everything I did and learned along the way prepared me to succeed in the role with stronger writing and editing skills.

Family and friends commented about how obvious it seemed that writing was what I should be doing. They asked why it took me so long to figure it out. More than a decade ago, I adopted a guiding principle to *solve no problem before its time*. As this tenet played out in my career transition, my problem wasn't solved until it was ready to be solved.

I certainly didn't enjoy feeling like a rat in a maze, running into walls of endless rejections and thwarted search directions. But it became crystal clear that *all* the exploration—with several dead ends and one huge mistake—helped me determine what kind of work I did, and did not, want to do. Every moment along the way mattered—rejections, obstacles, and victories. Each contributed in significant ways to learning and creating what came next.

✅ **TIP: Learn from *everything* on the road to your next destination.** While living through volatile ups and downs, wins and losses, we can be unaware of how much we're learning. Don't discount anything that happens along the way. Every moment is leading to your next chapter.

So Much to Do, So Little Time

One of my favorite lines from the PBS series, *Downton Abbey*, was when the Dowager Countess, played by Maggie Smith, asked "What is a weekend?" In the Downton context, weekends didn't exist for aristocrats who didn't work as we know it.

My weekends disappeared when I discovered my passion for writing and editing. Working seven days a week is my new normal, but it doesn't feel like work. It feels like my calling, exactly what I am meant to do. Whenever words are waiting to find their place on a page, I'm happy to be at my computer for hours on Saturdays and Sundays. Memoirs and books written by writers about writing have replaced novels as my favorite genres to read.

Doing what I love, I rarely have enough hours in the day. It's also true that "all work and no play" can make me a bit dull when I'm with other people. It's sometimes hard to shake myself out of writing mode to be present with others.

I must find ways to not overwork at the expense of relationships and taking care of myself. It's essential to create quality time with my husband and others I care about. And I know my brain needs and benefits from time and space away from my keyboard.

Finding My Purpose-Driven Calling

My purpose-driven calling came together as a business writer and editor, author, and catalyst for others navigating career transitions.

Below is a common illustration of how a clear purpose can be a unifying focal point for our lives and our work. It's magical when these come together as one—and we love what we do. I wish for you the joy of discovering what you are meant to do.

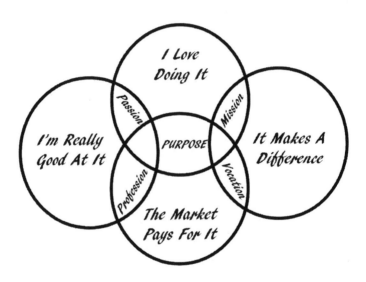

Discovering Your Next Chapter

Rather than having a preordained plan outside of our control, I believe we triumph when we do the work that sets the stage, and we are ready to handle what comes our way.

So, let's explore and discover what you *can* and *want* to do, and how to make it happen. The rest of the book focuses on your needs related to:

- Being a Hard-to-Define Professional
- Inventive Career Transitions
- Career Management Across Generations
- The Sweet Spot Job Search Method
- 25 Activities for Job Searching and Networking

PART III

THE ART OF INVENTIVE CAREER TRANSITIONS

*I find the harder I work, the
more luck I seem to have.*
— THOMAS JEFFERSON

Anatomy of a Hard-to-Define Professional

This section takes a closer look at what it means to be a Hard-to-Define Professional, why being one requires inventive job search methods, and how I became one.

Hard-to-Define Professionals share some or all of these characteristics:

- We've had one or more jobs that are hard to describe.

- Our transferable skills are not easily categorized into a single, clearly defined profession.

- We must be creative as we explore, discover, and describe what we *can* and *want* to do.

- It's hard to network productively when we aren't clear about what we *can* and *want* to do, and we don't have an elevator pitch that works.

- We struggle to articulate and sell our strengths and a distinct value proposition to prospective employers.

- It's challenging to secure roles that fit our sweet spot of capabilities, goals, and desires.

- Many of us want fulfilling, purpose-driven work in a place where we feel good about working. Finding a rare role can be more important than where it is, making it harder to develop a list of target organizations.

- We must learn how to conduct an atypical or inventive job search that results in interviews and offers—not résumés and applications that get lost in a black hole.

- Once we land in a new job, it's sometimes hard for colleagues to understand our capabilities so we are well situated and fully utilized.

Why Being a Hard-to-Define Professional Requires Inventive Career Transitions

Being Hard-to-Define has pros and cons. On the positive side, some people get the picture of all we can do. We are multifaceted with a treasure trove of skills we can apply in many situations. Because we're not pigeonholed in a clear profession, we can reinvent ourselves repeatedly as we find unusual roles we *can* and *want* to do.

On the flip side, we and others get confused about what we've done and what we *can* and *want* to do next. Much more than those who work in a distinct profession, we must master the art of describing and selling ourselves in different ways for different opportunities. The Sweet Spot Job Search Method in PART IV provides activities and tools to perform this art.

How I Became a Hard-to-Define Professional

All my professional roles have been unusual, with a wide variety of responsibilities. None were easily described as something I was looking for. I found these hidden gems by diligently mining hundreds of job ads, and landed them by marketing myself well. Each position was purposeful and satisfying in its own way.

In addition to a Swiss Army knife, I could describe myself as a chameleon, shape shifter, or serial transformer. As my recent job search moved in four directions, I felt like a magician saying: "Presto chango, now I'm a [fill in the blank]."

Retrospective:
My Hard-to-Define Career and Transitions

This retrospective begins in my youth and ends where I lost my job and began my reinvention. Connecting threads run through serious endeavors in my youth and my adult career as a Hard-to-Define Professional. These threads shed light on how I got where I am. Learning and growing in each role, I brought new aspects of myself to the next. More important than learning about *my* career, I hope you gain insights for navigating your own.

I Wanted to be a Ballet Dancer—Really!

Like many little girls across the globe, I began dance classes at age four. At age eight or nine, believing I had special talent, my ballet teacher suggested I audition at the School of American Ballet (SAB), the official school for the New York City Ballet (NYCB).

Two years later, I auditioned and was accepted to SAB. Eleven was old in ballet years to begin professional training. I took four to five dance classes each week, and had the magical experience of performing children's roles in several NYCB productions at Lincoln Center, including *The Nutcracker.*

The desire to dance and watch ballet permeated every cell of my being. For several years, I was committed to becoming a professional dancer. Unfortunately, in high school, my dream was crushed by the reality of not having enough talent or the right physique. But this childhood pursuit shaped many aspects of the rest of my life.

Rigorous training to become a professional dancer requires intense dedication, discipline, focus, fortitude, and perfectionism. Serious ballet students are hypercritical of themselves (and others). They never believe they are good enough—often leading to self-destructive thoughts and behaviors.

Consistent with OCD tendencies described in PART I: The Backstory, these characteristics still affect every facet of my life. The pros and cons of my desire to continually improve everything I do are always with me. Meticulous precision produces exceptional work products, but there comes a time to complete deliverables and move on—including writing and editing.

While I will always be captivated when watching talented dancers, I no longer enjoy dancing because my body can't produce the perfection my mind sees. Sadly, this tension became one reason I walked away from ballroom dancing with my husband—a special pastime we had shared for several years.

I Wanted to be a Psychologist

As my dancing dreams ended, the next phase of my career took shape. I got heavily involved in a high school peer-counseling program led by a psychologist. We had a "Rap Room" during the school year, and a summer program in which a cadre of students operated like mini-therapists. I seemed to have a knack for asking open-ended questions that guided my peers down a path of self-discovery.

Experiences with peer counseling and my own therapy left me determined to have a PhD in psychology by age 26. I majored in psychology at Clark University, known for being the only American graduate school where Sigmund Freud lectured.

As a college senior, I applied to more than 25 doctoral programs in psychology where admissions were more competitive than medical school. I declined one doctoral program in Michigan, and completed a master's degree in Psychological Services/Counseling Psychology at the University of Pennsylvania. Rather than pursuing a doctoral program right away, I decided to get some work experience.

My first job search entailed scouring the classified ads from A-to-Z in the Sunday newspaper. I found jobs to apply for throughout the ads—not only in the counselor or therapist categories. Unlike today's robust descriptions on job sites, companies paid by the word, and didn't spend a lot. The tiny print ads were about one inch wide by one to three inches long.

This section of the paper was delivered to my apartment on Saturdays, and I had a batch of envelopes (usually four to eight) in the mail by Sunday night. Each envelope included a standard résumé and a customized cover letter for each job as described in the ad.

After several months, I landed my first postgraduate job as a drug and alcohol prevention specialist at a state-funded youth service bureau. I created, marketed, and presented educational programs for students in kindergarten through eighth grade; provided individual, group, and family counseling; and taught an undergraduate course on drug and alcohol issues at Temple University.

At the end of three years, I was restless and ready for a change. I didn't want to start another school year of educational programs, and I was uncomfortable about being in a position to make decisions that affected clients' lives in significant ways.

While not always the case, many who choose to be therapists have worked through difficult issues of their own, and have a strong desire to help others do the same. Having resolved many issues in therapy, I no longer had a burning desire to help people work through their most personal issues. I wanted to transfer my skills to work with individuals and teams in business settings.

Against the Odds, I Transitioned to Business

Deciding to transition from nonprofit human services to business, I had no idea what that would look like, or how I would find my place in the vast, undefined world of "business."

A common reaction in conversations was that I wouldn't succeed in making the leap because I didn't have an MBA or any relevant experience. Lengthening my odds, many teachers and human services professionals (social workers and psychologists) were trying to transition into jobs in the business world.

Determined to make the switch, I lived on a monetary gift from my grandparents as an investment in my future. As in my previous search, I poured through the entire classified ads in the Sunday newspaper. Casting a wide net was even more important this time, because I had no idea what I was looking for.

Based on transferable skills I developed in graduate school and my first job, I looked at opportunities related to organizational development, training, and program management. Once again, I used a single résumé and a customized cover letter for each job I pursued.

After a nine-month search, I landed a terrific job as assistant director of a programmatic division of the Greater Philadelphia Chamber of Commerce. The eighth largest Chamber of Commerce in the U.S., this nonprofit business association was run much like a for-profit company. The program I co-led provided training and consulting services for executive teams implementing Total Quality Management (TQM), also known as Continuous Quality Improvement (CQI) in healthcare. Our services were based on the work of Dr. W. Edwards Deming, credited with helping the Japanese improve product quality after World War II. We worked with Dr. Deming and other quality-related thought leaders (including Tom Peters) to deliver programs and services for executives from every industry sector.

At the forefront of leadership practices, our work was purpose-driven. I enjoyed ongoing opportunities to learn about a wide range of businesses and business practices. It was like being in a never-ending MBA program. Broad responsibilities included program development, marketing, event management, and budgeting.

My bonus was meeting my husband who worked in the accounting department of the same organization. We met to correct an error in my first paycheck, enjoyed several picnic lunches and special dates, and developed our lifelong partnership. Together more than 30 years, we often joke about Bryan knowing I'm (almost) always right when I find a mistake.

After four years as assistant director, my boss was promoted to vice president and I became the program director. This was my first (and last) experience with managing employees, and I was miserable. Over the years, we had staff members who were exceptional to work with and became close friends. Others tested my performance management abilities, which I did not seem to possess.

Knowing a lot about leadership did not translate to being a good leader when employees were disengaged and interpersonal chemistry seemed to defy teamwork. Three years felt like an endless struggle with my accountability for the motivation, development, and performance of staff members who didn't seem to care. More than 20 years later, I continued to thrive as a collaborative individual contributor, leaving supervisory roles to others. Concerns about imposing my hypercritical perfectionism on others have contributed to this preference.

After seven years, I decided to leave at the end of a program year without having another job lined up. Fortunately, the president of the Chamber of Commerce had appreciated my contributions and valiantly looked out for me. He paved the way for me to stay while I pursued other opportunities.

Seeking a More Focused Role in One Company

Rather than continuing to provide services to many companies, I wanted an interesting and challenging job in one company. But I didn't want it to be as intense and consuming as my previous position. Despite an expanded array of transferable skills, I had no idea what my next role might be.

Yep, it was back to classified ads in the Sunday newspaper. As in previous searches, I used a single résumé with customized cover letters. After several months of searching, I was hired as assistant to the chief of staff at the company in which I worked for 20 years.

Because the interview process spanned several months, I went right from the Chamber to the new job. The chairman of the company that hired me was about to serve as chairman of the Chamber for the upcoming year. In addition to a strong résumé, cover letter, and interview, I was never sure whether this executive-level connection impacted my getting the job.

As described previously, my role evolved in many satisfying directions over 20 years. In my early fifties, I wanted to stay at the company as long as possible. Whenever I was ready to move toward retirement, I envisioned the possibility of transitioning to a part-time or consulting arrangement. As you know, this played out quite differently.

20 Great Years Minus 7 Days ... Now What?

This is where my story started. To recap in a nutshell, I lost a job I thought I wanted to keep, embarked on an odyssey to discover what I *could* and *wanted* to do next, conducted a successful 21st century job search, and launched my triumphant next chapter as a writer and editor.

Ironically, at age 56, I had become a more clearly defined professional than I had ever been. My reinvention created a new type of employability I could take with me wherever I went, for as long as I wanted to work.

Defining myself as a writer and editor, I would still use my Sweet Spot Job Search Method to find future full-time, part-time, or contract positions. Only certain writing and editing opportunities would be in my sweet spot, and I would continue to be selective.

Career Management Across Generations

Before examining the nuts and bolts of a masterful job search, I reflected on five topics relevant for your transition in the context of today's multigenerational workforce.

Layoffs were invented well before the most recent financial crisis. But prevalent employee views about employer/employee relationships and loyalty can be attributed to endless waves of downsizing since 2008.

While generational stereotypes suggest significant differences in attitudes about work, similarities far outweigh differences. Regardless of generation, many of us have the same concerns and care about the same things in relation to our work. Besides my thoughts and the citations that follow, "The Real Problem With Millennials at Work" is a great article on this topic (http://www.inc.com/david-burkus/the-real-problem-with-millennials-at-work.html).

1. Job Hopping: The New Normal for Everyone
Seeing and believing anyone could be laid off any time, many of us lost our sense of loyalty to employers. A "free-agent" mentality is prevalent among older workers who

have been laid off, and younger workers who enter the workforce expecting to change jobs numerous times. A common way of thinking is "happy to stay; ready to go"—prepared to market ourselves for new opportunities at a moment's notice.

According to 2014 data from the Bureau of Labor Statistics, median tenure with current employers was 4.6 years. While names and date ranges for generations vary by source, some studies reported that the majority of Millennials (born 1977-1998) expected to stay in their jobs less than three years. This means they could have 15 to 20 jobs during their careers. Baby Boomers (born 1946-1964) were reported to average 9.9 jobs between the ages of 25-48. Many changed jobs several times after age 48, perhaps after being laid off by one or more companies.

2. Contractor Mentality Goes Both Ways

With job security redefined, each of us must maintain our employability. Rather than expecting companies to employ us for life and manage our training and career development, it's up to us to take charge of our professional progression and keep our skills up to date.

Many companies are hesitant to add to their so-called permanent headcount, relying more heavily on contractors. Employers benefit from using contractors in many ways:

- Using contractors allows companies to more easily flex staffing levels up and down as business needs change. They can do this without the complexities that come with laying people off.

- Even before the Affordable Care Act (ACA) took effect in 2014, companies used contractors and part-time employees to avoid the high cost of health insurance premiums for full-time employees.

- Using contractors is a great way for companies to "try before they buy." They can test drive potential new hires to avoid mistakes—and employees can decide if the company is a place they want to work.

From the employee perspective, staying at one company for many years has become much more the exception than the norm. We avoid getting overinvested in long-term employment situations that could evaporate at any moment. An independent contractor mentality motivates many of us to add as much value as possible in each place we work.

In today's job market, we benefit from deciding where we sell our services as "Me, Inc." Portfolio careers with several concurrent employment arrangements are a growing trend. It's common to have a central anchor that provides steady income, with several satellite endeavors—freelance and/or contract assignments that change over time.

3. Importance of Purposeful Work and Flexibility Beats High Compensation Across Generations

Many leaders are attending to demographic shifts in the workforce. Some hire "Generational Consultants" to address a range of issues—real or imagined. Working Baby Boomers are often in a position to attract, engage, retain, communicate with, and leverage valuable capabilities of employees in their twenties and thirties.

Despite certain distinctions (e.g., comfort with technology), notable similarities across generations include a strong desire for meaningful, purpose-driven work in an organization we are proud of. Regardless of age, many employees want to do work that makes an important difference in other people's lives— maybe work that changes the world.

A common desire is to work for organizations that give us flexibility to get the job done when and where we want to work. Staying connected and collaborating through technology has blurred lines of distinction between work and personal time. Lack of clear boundaries is increasingly common and accepted (even expected) among employees of all ages. As an aside, many of us could benefit from rethinking aspects of how perpetually connected we are.

The concept of work/life flexibility makes more sense to me than work/life balance. Assuming professionals are dedicated to doing whatever it takes to get the job done, circumstances dictate when work or life outside of work needs more attention. Especially for jobs that don't require set schedules, the ability to responsibly manage shifting priorities in and out of work is priceless.

4. Midlife Career Transitions: Getting Hired at Age 50+/-

Many midlife job seekers are convinced they won't get hired because of their age. Some give up and stop trying. Being over age 50 could add time to your search, but it is *not* a showstopper.

Just like I never gave a moment's thought to how being a woman might hinder my professional goals, I never gave this age-based notion any power to get in my way. Looking and sounding younger than my age, and not aspiring to senior executive roles might have been advantages for me. But many people in my network have landed jobs in their fifties and sixties.

How you think about your age will affect how you approach your job search and the results you achieve. If you perceive your age as a barrier, it will be. If you perceive your age as a non-issue, it will be. Applying this to your job search is a powerful place to operate from.

But let's look at some age-related dynamics that could come into play during a midlife career transition. A common assumption is that companies prefer to hire younger, less expensive employees. Wherever this age bias might be true, employers are walking away from talented, experienced professionals who could be invaluable assets to their businesses.

On the other hand, some older workers have or will become technology dinosaurs as Millennials and subsequent digital-native generations overtake the workforce. We all know the velocity of technology innovations is accelerating exponentially.

Some Baby Boomers resist or find it difficult to keep up with mobile devices, social media, and related communication practices that emerge and disappear at an ever-faster pace. People in this age range are especially challenged if they never developed the intuitive ability to find their way around new devices, software, social media, the cloud, and whatever else comes next. With many accessible ways to keep technology skills current, it's up to us to do so.

If you are older than 45, it might be wise to defend against potential hiring biases by age proofing your résumé, LinkedIn profile, and online applications. It's easy to do by omitting dates on educational degrees and excluding one or more early jobs. However, if your longer history tells an impressive story relevant to your search objectives, it's not necessary to include only the most recent 15 years' experience in your résumé and other profiles. There's more to come on this in Part IV: Sweet Spot Job Search Method and 25 Activities.

5. Encore Careers

Moving further away from the false positive job I left after eight days, I gained additional clarity about the type of work I did and did not want to do. Still energized and committed to work long and hard when it made an important difference to those it touched, I became more selective about the jobs I pursued.

When I saw occasional job postings for a chief of staff or special assistant to CEO, I still looked, but turned away with surety it was no longer a good fit. It became crystal clear that I wanted to write and edit content that was meaningful to others and satisfying for me.

For many Baby Boomers, replicating a previous job and compensation level can become less realistic—perhaps less desirable. Rather than working to have the resources we need to live, Boomers might be ready and able to choose work we love (often referred to as living to work vs. working to live).

One notion is to determine your income requirement, find (hopefully satisfying) work to meet that requirement, and do other work because you want to—not because you have to or think you should. If financial conditions allow (including family obligations and retirement scenarios), and you can afford to earn less than before, a midlife transition can be a well-earned opportunity to downshift from high-pressure corporate jobs, and find purpose-driven work you enjoy.

Countless books and articles have been written about evolving definitions of retirement. It's increasingly common for people to gradually transition away from demanding full-time work, while adding more purposeful and satisfying "encore" careers, volunteer commitments, and leisure activities. It can be a first step toward whatever "retirement" looks like. Blog posts on this topic by Dave Bernard are well worth reading (http://www.usnews.com/topics/author/dave-bernard).

As my husband and I reached midlife, more people we knew became critically ill and/or passed away—some far too young. During my editing contract, my husband was diagnosed and began chemotherapy for a rare but curable form of Hodgkin's lymphoma. So there we were, confronted by a serious illness in our fifties. Thankfully, his treatment and prognosis were favorable. But this was a loud and clear wakeup call to enjoy our lives as much as possible while we could.

Even with my husband's illness, my prolonged period of unemployment proved I was nowhere near as ready to retire as I thought I would be at this age. Past yearnings to retire significantly younger than age 65 disappeared. I emerged on the other side of this job loss tunnel with my calling—work I will probably want and need to do far into the future. Fortunately, Sententia can join me to compose and edit on my keyboard wherever I am.

Now it's time to dive into the resources you need to invent your next chapter.

PART IV

SWEET SPOT JOB SEARCH METHOD

*Saying "No" gives us space to
focus on what's important.*

Each person has their own definition of a sweet spot job.
Many would call it their dream job, their passion, or their calling. Whatever you call it, figuring out what you *don't* want to
do is just as important as discovering what you *want* to do
and why.

With the time and energy you spend working, you owe it to
yourself to feel great about your work. The more you do things
you don't want to do, the less time you have to do what's important to you. Saying "No" might include turning down jobs
that are not in your sweet spot.

With a job search done well you are likely to have choices,
which means you don't have to accept offers that don't match
most or all of your sweet spot criteria. Making intentional decisions

increases your chances of thriving far beyond 18 months and being fulfilled by work you care about—a lot.

The more fully a job meets my three sweet spot criteria, the sweeter it is:

1. **Work I *can* do in my Capability Zone.** This work leverages the things I do best. Even if it's a big stretch out of my comfort zone, I'm confident I will ultimately add value and succeed. The next section expands on this concept.

2. **Work I *want* to do.** I aim to do work I *care* about because it makes an important difference to those it touches, and work I *enjoy* because it calls on strengths I like to use. Far beyond a paycheck, I've always looked for meaningful work.

3. **Work in a purpose- and values-driven organization.** I seek jobs in organizations with a purpose I find compelling and values consistent with my own. Pride and comfort in how the organization operates has always been important. Even if a job matches my other criteria, there are places I would never work because there's a gap between my values and how the organization operates.

The Sweet Spot Job Search Method is a significant departure from prevailing advice. We've established that job seekers are advised to spend 80% to 90% of their time networking because it's *the* most important activity and how they are most likely to land their next job.

My contrasting view is that, rather than focusing only or primarily on networking, you increase your chances for a successful career transition by implementing an effective combination of three elements, in this order:

1. **Diligent Online Keyword Searches, Daily Alerts, and Applications.** This process can help you decide and articulate what you *can* and *want* to do; then find, apply, interview, and land those sweet spot jobs. The power of doing this well is vastly underestimated.

2. **Superior Marketing Materials.** Successful online applications require exceptional résumé(s), cover letters, LinkedIn profiles, etc.

3. **Networking With Purpose.** Focusing on quality vs. quantity means connecting and establishing relationships with individuals for specific reasons, with thoughtful preparation and follow up.

Sweet Spot Funnel

The Sweet Spot Job Search Method (the Method) is based on a funnel concept that begins with considering divergent possibilities in the early stages, and gradually converging on a narrower set of options. It involves casting a wide net at the top of the funnel and working your way down to focus on a narrower range of sweet spot opportunities at the bottom. Following the process over time generates opportunities that fulfill your needs, preferences, and aspirations. The ultimate outcome is finding work you love.

This illustration shows the elements of the Method. The top-to-bottom order and relative size of the circles in the Funnel are intentional:

Sweet Spot Funnel

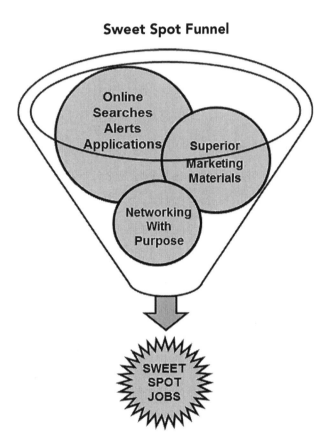

By implementing the 25 Activities embedded in this framework, you can achieve many important objectives:

- Explore a broad array of possible career directions without imposing limits on what you consider

- Discover a wider variety of opportunities that might be a fit; open your mind to shifting gears
- Crystallize key capabilities and strengths you enjoy and would like to continue using in your work
- Zero in to pursue one or more search strategies in your target location(s)
- Define a distinct value proposition that positions your experience and transferable skills to fit the roles you want to pursue
- Easily customize résumés and cover letters more likely to land in the "Yes" pile for interviews
- Apply selectively to generate interviews and offers for sweet spot jobs

The Method begins by experimenting with searches using a wide variety of keywords in the *job title* field that describe work you might enjoy. It's best to *not* limit initial searches to your geographic region. This expands possibilities for roles that could be a fit. Later, you will narrow your search to pursue one or more clear directions within your target location(s), and then find and apply for opportunities that interest you.

As you find interesting jobs in any location, capture keywords and phrases that match what you *can* and might *want* to do in your next position. You will use these to create your LinkedIn profile, résumé, and customized cover letters. These steps are explained fully in 25 Activities.

Capability Zone

We learn and grow wiser from each challenge we conquer, those we don't, and those we wish would have played out differently.

When searching for jobs, I pursue new challenges that allow me to stretch, learn, and grow. But I avoid stretching too far by taking on roles in which I believe I won't ever meet my high performance standards. I intentionally stay within my Capability Zone.

I thrive when I work within my Capability Zone, and my life is enriched as new challenges expand its boundaries. Here are additional thoughts and an illustration of three zones in relation to job searches, work, and life:

Comfort Zone. I know I am more than capable to add value and succeed. Once I know how to do everything I need to deliver, this is the most limiting place to stay. At this stage of my career, a pure proofreading job would fit in this category.

Capability Zone. This is work I *can* and *want* to do. Even if I've never done exactly what the job calls for, it feels like work I am wired to do—it's in my wheelhouse. If I'm confident I will ultimately add value and succeed, I make a commitment and persevere to conquer challenges. Stretching beyond perceived limits expands the margins of my Capability Zone.

When these factors exist in a place I *want* to work, I operate at my best and deliver exceptional quality. My triumphant writing and editing job is a great example of a job in this category.

Don't-Go-There Zone. With no related experience or confidence in my ability to add value and succeed, I don't pursue jobs in this category. These jobs are not in my wheelhouse.

They are outside of what I *want* or believe I am wired to do. For example, I would not pursue a role responsible for mergers and acquisitions, pharmaceutical R&D, finance, or an entire marketing, sales, service, or HR function.

Capability Zone

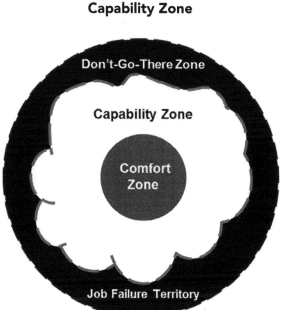

Reasons to Job Search in Your Capability Zone

In contrast to staying within their Capability Zone, some job seekers are advised to apply freely, even if they don't come close to meeting requirements in job descriptions. I've heard people tell job seekers to sell themselves aggressively to get offers, and later say "Thanks, but no thanks," and walk away—which they knew they would do from the beginning.

Many people thrive and urge others to take on roles that stretch them far beyond what they believe they can deliver.

Within the job search context, it can be a risky proposition for both candidates and employers when applicants reach beyond their Capability Zones. While you might need to *fake it 'til you make it* in this zone, you are more likely to *fake it 'til you fail* in your Don't-Go-There Zone. Pursuing opportunities in the Don't-Go-There Zone contributes to far too many unqualified applicants for each job, and the abysmal success rate for new hires discussed in the insights about the broken interview process. Washing out within 18 months can happen when people apply and sell themselves into jobs they have never done, are not qualified for, and will never do well.

An example of staying in my Capability Zone was not pursuing chief of staff or special assistant to CEO roles in global, publicly traded, manufacturing companies. I did not believe I had the experience to make these a sweet spot match.

I've sometimes wondered whether self-doubt caused me to underestimate my abilities and miss opportunities to take on challenges I could conquer. Others have said I stayed too safe and aimed too low. Sometimes criticized for taking on only work I wanted to do, I always viewed my choices as wisely selective so I would be successful and fulfilled by doing what I did best and enjoyed most.

In a career management classic, *Who's Hiring Who*, Richard Lathrop observed that the person who gets hired is often not the best fit for the job, but the one who knows how to get hired. Unfortunately, my false positive experience fit this scenario.

In my perfect world, the one who gets hired is the person who can best do the job *and* knows how to get hired. In the 2014 edition of *What Color is Your Parachute: Guide to Rethinking Resumes*, Richard N. Bolles sites the appalling statistic that job hunters spend only 60 seconds reading a job description before deciding to apply. This drives another problematic statistic that the average job posting receives 250 résumés, and many receive hundreds more.

This activity by job seekers puts us all in a bad place. It could be a big factor in why so many résumés are never seen by a person. And those that are, receive only four to eight seconds of attention before landing in the "Yes" or "No" pile for further consideration.

Outside the sphere of career transitions, in other aspects of life and work, it's exhilarating to venture into new territory and accomplish great things you never imagined. Pushing beyond perceived abilities is a key principle in the consulting firm where I landed my writing and editing job. I'm learning about the power of reaching beyond your experience to achieve things you never thought you could. Once you're in a sweet spot job you love, go for it. Push the boundaries of your Capability Zone—reach for the stars!

But back in job search mode, the interview process is a two-way street. Both sides should conduct thorough due diligence to ensure a good match within the candidate's Capability Zone.

25 Activities:
Most and Least Helpful for
Job Searching and Networking

Luck is what happens when
preparation meets opportunity.
— LUCIUS ANNAEUS SENECA

These 25 Activities are organized in the general sequence I developed and used them. Rather than a linear progression, many activities are iterative and concurrent as a job search unfolds. Your sequence and pace depends on your situation and readiness for each step.

While I'm sharing what did and didn't work well for me, your experience might differ. Even as best practices for job search evolve quickly, many of these activities and tools will stand the test of time and provide useful references as you invent your own next chapter.

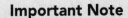

Important Note

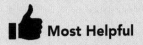 **Most Helpful**   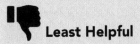 **Least Helpful**

Each Activity includes methods and tools I found most and least helpful. The *least helpful* sections begin with common recommendations shown in bold, followed by my differing experiences and points of view.

25 Activities List

Activity 1
Self-Assessments

Career coaching often begins with several self-assessments. Some are industry standards; others are created by individual coaches. The intent is to help clients discover strengths, preferences, and the purpose or passion they would ideally like to fulfill through their work.

Self-discovery is essential for Hard-to-Define Professionals, anyone considering a directional shift, and anyone who wants to explore possibilities to find deeply satisfying work—perhaps their dream job.

 **Self-Assessments: Most Helpful**

Self-Discovery for Inventive Career Transitions. Completing a few worksheets helped me gain clarity about what was more and less important in my next job. I created a comprehensive worksheet to help you explore and discover what's most important and compelling for you in your next chapter (Sample 1).

 **Self-Assessments: Least Helpful**

Myers Briggs Type Indicator (MBTI). This is one of the most widely used and validated personality assessment instruments. Reviewing a previous or new MBTI report could help your coach understand what makes you tick. A report can provide interesting insights about your styles and preferences for interacting with your world. However, it didn't help me figure out what I wanted to do with my career.

Strengthsfinder 2.0. This is an industry gold standard to identify your strengths and types of work that would be most satisfying. Taking the assessment and studying the results on my own didn't increase my understanding of my strengths, what I wanted to do, or how to describe myself. Perhaps I would have found my path sooner with expert guidance to interpret my report.

Activity 2
Accomplishment Stories:
Problem, Action, Results, Skills (PARS)
Situation, Action, Results, Skills (SARS)
Situation, Task, Action, Results (STAR)

Whatever you call them, these are written examples of how you solved a problem or added value in the past. These accomplishments provide fuel for your résumé and answers to behavioral interview questions.

 **Accomplishment Stories: Most Helpful**

Keep them short and sweet. Make these short and concise (three to five sentences) so you can leverage them in résumé bullets and responses to interview questions. Describe a snapshot of the situation in just enough detail for your audience to "get it" and understand the rest of your story. You might develop some in greater detail to prepare for specific interviews.

Write these early in your transition. Develop these early in your transition to recall significant accomplishments and regain confidence in your abilities.

Accomplishment Stories: Least Helpful

Write one-page stories. Writing one-page narratives made them too long and, therefore, less useful as input for my résumé bullets and interview responses.

Activity 3
Online Job Searches and Daily Alerts

We've established that investing significant time in online searches and applications is a key difference between my job search methods and commonly prescribed networking-based approaches. Today's robust job postings provide a wealth of information to address in your marketing documents and interview preparation.

 Online Job Searches: Most Helpful

Online job postings. Three types of job sites were prevalent during my search. Others were emerging quickly, so this is an area to monitor closely.

1. **Job Search Consolidation Engines.** Indeed, ZipRecruiter, SimplyHired, etc.

2. **Branded Job Boards.** LinkedIn, CareerBuilder, Monster, Glassdoor, Craigslist, etc.

3. **Company Career Website Pages.** Many job postings in #1 and #2 redirect you to apply on company career pages—the best places to do so. When you identify target companies,

search and set up alerts on their career pages for jobs that fit your criteria.

Job website profiles and résumé uploads. Stay informed as the most popular websites in #1 and #2 (above) evolve. Both types of online job sites allow you to create profiles and upload résumés. Whenever a profile parses information from your résumé, it requires significant manipulation to get the right information in the right places. Don't skip this step, which can be time consuming.

One-click applications. Many social media platforms (e.g., Twitter, Facebook, and others that don't yet exist) are gaining ground quickly in the recruiting game. Proceed with caution as job websites and social media platforms allow you to use profiles and uploaded résumés to apply with one click from mobile and other devices. Applying this way prevents you from customizing a cover letter or anything else you submit. But stay tuned—cover letters could become extinct if one-click applications take over.

Recommended job boards. Besides LinkedIn, choose two or three job search consolidators or branded job boards to search and, when ready, set up daily alerts. As mentioned previously, Indeed was the search engine that worked best for me. Online resources continue to evolve, and what works best for you could vary based on your geographic location and search strategies.

Paid memberships and subscriptions. Other than membership fees for career-specific associations, don't pay for job board subscriptions or to gain access to apply for a job. You can probably find the same jobs on free job boards and/or directly through company websites.

Specialized websites. Use free job boards offered by nonprofits and professional associations, e.g.:

- **Nonprofits:** idealist.org, philanthropy.com, workforgood. org (formerly OpportunityKnocks)
- **Associations:** American Society for Association Executives (careerhq.asaeconter.org/jobs)
- **Education:** National Association of Independent Schools (nais.org.), chroniclevitae.com, higheredjobs.com

Master the Sweet Spot Job Search Method to cast a wide net for keyword searches. Leverage this essential job search activity for any Inventive Career Transition (i.e., Hard-to-Define Professionals, not sure what you want to do next, switching careers). It also works if you are looking for a specific type of position. These details build on the earlier introduction of the Method:

- Attend a free LinkedIn webinar if you don't know how to conduct keyword searches. Transfer the knowledge to other job search engines and job boards.

- Experiment with combinations of words in the *job title* field. Search functions on job boards respond differently to using "and" and "or" between keywords and quotation marks around them.

- Early in your search, be playful and experiment with a wide range of filters and search parameters. Start with divergent ideas to consider an expansive array of possibilities. Over time, narrow your funnel and converge on a shorter list for saved searches and daily alerts.

- Your goal is to develop a list of titles to monitor and pursue over time:
  - Begin by searching for generic titles (e.g., coordinator, specialist, communications, executive, program manager, project manager) that can apply to a wide range of organizations and industries.
  - Don't limit early searches to your geographic area while you explore and learn about new possibilities.
  - Later, when you know what you're looking for, zero in on your target location(s). When I knew what kind of jobs I wanted to focus on, I saved searches using my zip code plus a 25-mile radius.

Saved searches and daily alerts. Invest time to perform this vital activity. Once you save searches, search engines and job boards are fairly accurate in showing you only the new postings and recommendations since the last time you looked.

- Be diligent (in my case, obsessed) about reviewing daily alerts. I got fast at screening hundreds of jobs each day based on titles and one or two lines of text. I could go several days finding nothing to apply for, then find a few on another day—including weekends, holidays, and all summer.

- Apply quickly (ideally the same day) to a new job posting to increase your chances of getting noticed.

Activity 4
Departure Statement

This is a carefully crafted answer to the inevitable question about why you are no longer in your previous job. These tips are most relevant if your position was involuntarily terminated.

After I gave one of the sample answers below, I was never asked a follow-up question.

 **Departure Statement: Most Helpful**

Don't volunteer this statement unless asked. There is no need to bring this up unless someone asks why you are no longer at your prior company.

Tell the truth, but not the whole truth. Develop a concise, partial answer. It must be true, but it should not be the whole story if that could put you or your previous employer in a negative light.

Don't vent. Regardless of what happened when you lost your job, don't speak negatively about your previous employer(s). Don't let negative feelings come through in what you say or how you say it.

End on a positive note. If asked why you are in transition, respond briefly, then shift to a positive statement about what you accomplished in your previous role(s) and what you want to do next. Don't leave your departure statement hanging in an uncomfortable silence that invites additional questions.

Sample Departure Statements:

Mention of job elimination. "There was a major reorganization, and [#] jobs were eliminated. Unfortunately, mine was one of them. But I had a great [#]-year run at the company, and I'm ready for new opportunities."

No mention of job elimination. "There was a major organizational change, so I took this great opportunity to pursue my long-term dream of [fill in the blank with what you're pursuing that fits the conversation you are in]."

Fill the employment gap. Find credible and creative ways to say you've been doing freelance work during your transition. It's irrelevant to differentiate whether you were paid or volunteered. Having interim work on your résumé plays well and can make your job loss a non-issue. Showing initiative to freelance might give you points, especially if someone has an outdated bias to not hire anyone who is unemployed for any reason (Activity 17: Reasons to Volunteer; Activity 18: Alternative Work Arrangements).

Activity 5
Elevator Pitch

Not to be confused with your departure statement, this is your carefully crafted answer when someone asks, "Tell me about yourself. What do you do?" Common advice is to use different versions in different situations (e.g., 30 seconds and two to three minutes). The more clearly defined your search strategy, the easier this is to create. Crafting this can be challenging and iterative, especially if you are exploring multiple directions.

 **Elevator Pitch: Most Helpful**

Emphasize your value; not your title. Rather than stating your most recent or target title(s), focus on the value you provide and what you want to do in your next job. Create a value proposition that explains how you help companies or clients. It's even better if you can include how you increase revenue and/or reduce costs. We'll talk more about this in Activity 6: Professional Brand.

Define your target role(s). Clearly explain what you want to do in your next job. This can vary based on the conversation you're in, and evolve as your search continues.

Sound natural. Ensure that what you put on paper comes out of your mouth sounding like you. Versions of your elevator pitch will become a key part of your interview strategy.

Activity 6
Professional Brand

More powerful than an elevator pitch, a professional brand describes your distinct value proposition in a way that helps people remember you and what you can do for them. Like your elevator pitch, it's important for this to sound natural when people ask you to tell them about yourself.

 Professional Brand: Most Helpful

Why should an employer choose you? In conversations, aim to use seven words or less to describe your core value proposition—how you help people or companies. I've heard this kind of branding statement referred to as a "memory dart" by Eric Kramer (www.interviewbest.com), and a "money shot" by Matt Levy, another career coach. Whatever you call it, it must be something you can easily repeat in conversations that helps people remember you.

Marketing tagline. In print, aim to use six words or less to describe the value you deliver. This could become a tagline in your marketing materials (e.g., résumé, LinkedIn profile, business cards).

These are examples of branding statements and tag lines I evolved for two search strategies.

For Chief of Staff | Special Assistant to CEO

- **Conversational introduction:** I work with CEOs and executive teams as a trusted partner, catalyst, communicator, and facilitator.
- **Headline on résumé and LinkedIn profile:** Trusted Partner | Catalyst | Communicator | Facilitator
- **Other concepts I played with but didn't use:** Swiss Army Knife, Woman or Wizard Behind the Curtain, Wingman (Woman), Assist Maker

For Writer | Editor | Proofreader

- **Conversational introduction:** I'm a writer and editor who helps people perfect their words.
- **Business name and website:** WordsPerfected, LLC (www. WordsPerfected.net)
- **Website and business card taglines:**
  - Your Words Perfected
  - … from letters on a keyboard to a symphony of words
  - I Perfect Words. Clients Get Results.
- **Résumé tagline:** Ideas, words, grammar, and format perfected!

Activity 7
Business Cards

Whether or not you pursue freelance endeavors, you need business cards for networking. The minimum to include is your contact information. Business cards range from simple, do-it-yourself to professionally designed, with or without a company logo. I started with the former and evolved to the latter.

 Business Cards: Most Helpful

Be creative and memorable. Replace or complement previous and target titles to promote what's special about you. As described above, use a memorable brand or tagline (six words or less) that articulates the value you provide. It's great if this matches your LinkedIn and résumé headlines.

Consider using a memorable image to keep you front of mind for the right opportunities. Use images available at no cost in the public domain, or pay for copyrighted images. Among many online sources, you can find both types of images at www.bing.com/images.

Do It Yourself (DIY) while exploring different search strategies. Use an Avery template for "Clean Edge Business Cards" if you need time to refine your story and search objective(s). While developing endless iterations of my business cards (surprised?), I did not invest in getting them professionally printed.

Have cards printed professionally once you decide how to market yourself. Choose a print vendor once you know what you want your cards to say about you. Office supply chains and online companies create business cards with options to use their templates and designs or upload your own. Vistaprint (www.vistaprint.com) produces attractive cards, and I became a delighted customer of www.Moo.com.

Decide how to use both sides. Choose paper with a flat finish on one side (usually the back) so people can write notes to remember how they met you and how they plan to follow up. Common advice is to take advantage of both sides to tell your story, leaving enough space for people to write notes.

Activity 8
LinkedIn Profile and Connections

Leveraging LinkedIn with a strong profile is essential for most professionals, particularly those in transition. Recruiting professionals usually search candidates' online presence during the screening process. LinkedIn, Twitter, and Facebook accounts are commonly checked.

The variety of social media platforms is expanding quickly, and each will become more or less important for career management over time. While completing this, Microsoft acquired LinkedIn and several start-ups were creating competing platforms.

There are as many opinions about how to write an effective LinkedIn profile as there are about résumés. This section focuses on creating a strong profile and building your connections. Activity 13: Networking With Purpose, includes a more in-depth discussion about using LinkedIn for productive networking.

LinkedIn continually changes features and functions without notice to users. On any given day, you might have to relearn how to do something you knew how to do the day before. Some changes can be frustrating and interfere with how you want to use the platform.

 **LinkedIn Profile: Most Helpful**

Attend a LinkedIn overview. When new to LinkedIn, attend a free, introductory webinar on how to create a strong profile. Also attend educational sessions at your local library or career networking groups.

Manage privacy settings. Lock down your privacy settings while you create and edit your profile. This allows you to view other profiles anonymously and change yours without notifying your network.

Manage "Privacy & Settings" by placing your cursor on the tiny version of your photo (or photo placeholder) in the top right corner of your profile. Work through each question in each section to manage who can see each aspect of your profile. When your profile is in good shape for others to see, change your settings to make more of it visible to more people.

Find great profiles to emulate. See how others describe themselves in ways you do and don't want to imitate. Consider profiles of people with job titles you are interested in and others you respect.

Choose your photo wisely. Post a photo before inviting people to connect. A studio-quality portrait isn't necessary, but you must look professional—probably not a close-up facial shot. Pay attention to what shows in the background.

A flattering color in your clothing and/or a frame can help your photo pop; however, framed photos can be tricky to manipulate in the space provided. Black-and-white photos are also effective.

Develop a distinctive headline. Optimize and leverage this prime real estate right under your name. Use all available characters to define your value proposition (brand), and entice people to keep reading. Don't limit your headline to past, present, or target titles.

To increase your chances of being found in a search, experiment with creative ways to combine *target* titles with the value you bring to targeted role(s). Use vertical pipes ("|") to separate elements and make sure the lines break in a way that makes sense. Find and replicate examples you like.

Select your industry with intention. LinkedIn defaults to your most recent industry based on the jobs in your Experience section. You can—and absolutely should—change this if you want to make a career change. Your selection should be a credible description of your experience and capabilities, and position you toward where you want to go.

Searching on this field is a key way people find certain types of professionals. You must choose from the dropdown list that's long enough to find something that's a reasonably good fit with where you're heading.

Because I did not want to stay in financial services, I experimented with several options. As my direction shifted, I looked at people in interesting jobs to help me select an industry. Over time, my choices included Management Consulting, Program Management, Executive Office, Writing and Editing.

Broaden your geographic location to match the radius of your search and desired commute. LinkedIn enters a default location based on your zip code. You can and should modify this to represent where you want to work. Increase flexibility by listing a geographic region rather than a specific city or town.

Provide detailed contact information. Make it easy for people to reach you by providing contact information in three places:

- **LinkedIn URL.** Customize your default URL with a simple version of your name by clicking on the small blue wheel that appears next to the default URL under your photo.

- **Contact Information.** Under your photo, provide your personal email address and/or cell phone number if you want people to reach you directly without going through LinkedIn. Include a company and/or personal website link if you want people to view them.

- **Advice for Contacting.** Make it extra easy for people to reach you by including your contact information in this section of Additional Information. Some people add a note about how they prefer to be contacted.

Craft a good summary. Maximize the value of this prime real estate. Some recommend using all available space; others recommend keeping it short and sweet. Repeat keywords for targeted roles to show up higher in search results. The top one-third of your résumé is a great source for this content and they should be consistent.

Write your profile in first or third person. This a personal decision with no right or wrong answer. I went back and forth several times (surprised again?), ending up with a more personal first-person voice in my LinkedIn summary and website bio. I used a third-person voice for my résumé and LinkedIn experience section.

Showcase your work experience. Mirror parts of your résumé during your job search. I repeated a lot of information from my résumé and didn't shy away from having an in-depth profile. Common advice is to keep this short so people ask for your complete résumé. I wrote a short paragraph and accomplishment-based bullets for each position.

Many recommend including only the past 10 to 15 years of work experience, especially if you are age 50+/- and want to age-proof job applications. Even if you include a longer history on your résumé, it's valid to use a shorter version for LinkedIn and online job applications (Activity 11). It's also fine to include a complete work history if it demonstrates your strong fit with target opportunities.

Rather than listing each title you had in the same organization as a separate job, develop a single entry for each company that includes your full tenure and most recent title. You can also list all titles in reverse chronological order in the text.

Acquire substantive recommendations. Aim for at least three to five solid recommendations. Getting this done can require care and feeding. It's helpful to offer to return the favor when you ask for these. It's also wise to offer to draft points or even the full copy you would like people to emphasize. Many people appreciate your making their job easier. Since you must accept and post what they write, you can ask for revisions, but this can become awkward. If these are strong, use them to create a testimonials document (Activity 24: References and Testimonials).

Use the Skills & Endorsements section wisely. Consider carefully whether and how you use this section of your profile. My appreciation for the credibility and value of this information declined when I received multiple endorsements for a skill I had no desire to include. Wondering how people received over 100 endorsements on skills without making it a full-time job, I concluded many came from people who didn't know much about the person they were endorsing. Valid or not, getting hundreds of endorsements requires significant care and feeding, and seems like an "I'll scratch your back if you'll scratch mine" activity.

If you don't have the time or inclination to give and get a lot of endorsements, you can exclude this section from your profile, or simply list your top 10-20 skills and opt out of receiving endorsements. People often include the maximum number of skills, but it's rare to get endorsements beyond the first 20 that show up without clicking "more"—and few people look beyond here.

Despite my cynicism, having many endorsements on skills that match targeted jobs could increase your keyword density so you rank higher in search results. It might also give you an advantage among similarly qualified candidates.

Include all secondary education. List graduate and undergraduate schools, degrees, and certifications in reverse chronological order. Omit dates if you are age 50+/-. The most impressive school should appear in the top section of your profile; add advanced credentials to your name (e.g., MBA, MSW, RN, PhD).

Skip paying for a premium or job seeker upgrade. Save your money, especially while you're not earning an income. Once my job search was in high gear, I upgraded to a Premium/Job Seeker account. After several months, I concluded it was not worth the monthly fee for these reasons:

- **Display of everyone who viewed your profile.** With a free account, you can see seven people who most recently viewed your profile. This is valuable and adequate if you check your profile frequently.

- **Three InMail messages per month.** These got a lower response rate than standard, free invitations to connect.

- **Featured applicant.** According to LinkedIn, this gets you to the top of the applicant list. I got better results by finding first-degree connections who introduced me to people in companies where I applied.

- **Applicant insights.** LinkedIn shows whether you are in the top or bottom 10%, 25%, or 50% of the applicant pool by using algorithms that compare keywords in your profile and the job description. LinkedIn also provides average salaries for similar jobs. I paid little attention to these features when deciding whether to pursue an opportunity.

 **LinkedIn Connections: Most Helpful**

Connect with purpose. Begin with a minimum of 50 first-degree connections and expand your network over time. Focusing on quality vs. quantity, I connect when I have a genuine reason based on how we might help each other now or in the future. I call this networking or connecting with purpose, and wrote about it in detail (Activity 13: Networking With Purpose).

Always send personalized invitations. Write a personalized note every time you invite someone to connect. Never use the boilerplate invitation messages embedded in LinkedIn.

Certain changes made it more difficult to find the option write personal notes when sending and receiving invitations. New settings defaulted to boilerplate invitations and "✓" to accept or "X" to decline invitations. Are you kidding me?

Respond to boilerplate invitations with a personalized note. Encourage others to connect with purpose. It's particularly annoying to receive an invitation when the person hasn't even looked at my profile. When I receive a boilerplate invitation to connect with someone I've never met, I usually send a message along these lines:

"Thanks for your invitation to connect. It would be helpful to know how you found me and how you think we might be able to help each other. I look forward to hearing about potential shared interests." If no response, I conclude there wasn't any reason for us to connect.

Invite job interviewers to connect. Decide whether to invite interviewers to connect before or after your interview. At a minimum, view their profile(s) before you meet by phone or in person. Interviewers might be more willing to accept your invitation after your conversation.

Even when you don't get a job, connect with people who interviewed you. As previously mentioned, getting a "No" might not be the forever answer. If you were a strong candidate, you might have another chance if the job reopens.

Having this first-degree connection can be especially helpful in these situations.

 **LinkedIn Connections: Least Helpful**

Have 500+ connections. Common advice is to connect with as many people as you can. Why? What's the value in connecting with people you know nothing about, other than (maybe) viewing their profile, and don't contact for a specific reason?

While large networks can be valuable, connecting with everyone who breathes to make your network as large as possible makes no sense. It's common to ask a person with 500+ connections to introduce you to one of their first-degree connections, only to hear they have no idea who the person is or where they met them. They might not even know if the person is male or female.

Even worse, some people have promoted shortcuts to appear as though you viewed hundreds of profiles without actually doing so. They did this because viewing others attracts reciprocal views and invitations, and raises certain profile rankings. I viewed this as the antithesis of networking with purpose. I heard that LinkedIn caught on to these tricks and cut people off when they exceeded reasonable thresholds of networking activity.

Send boilerplate invitations to connect. As noted, LinkedIn made it more difficult to write personalized notes when sending and receiving invitations. I urge you to learn how—and do it every time. The only exceptions might be when you work with someone, or if you had an in-depth conversation and agreed to connect without taking time to write a note.

Download contacts to LinkedIn. *Don't do this!* If you provide access, LinkedIn sends automatic, boilerplate invitations to everyone in your contact database.

Activity 9
Résumé(s)

Your résumé has four to eight seconds to grab someone's attention.

There are probably more varied opinions about résumés than any other item in your job search toolkit. No single formula works for every situation. Monitor evolving best practices because an exceptionally well-crafted résumé is an essential element of your marketing materials. Hiring an experienced résumé writer can make a big difference in the quality and efficacy of your document. If you don't hire a professional, it's critical to have someone with an eagle eye proofread it thoroughly for spelling, grammar, and punctuation before you use it. Errors can put your résumé in the fast lane to the "No" pile.

Notice this is not activity number one. I needed to do a *lot* of background work before I was ready to tackle my résumé—particularly because it hadn't been updated for 20 years. We've established that I made endless revisions to my marketing documents, especially as my search strategies shifted. In the early months of my transition, when people said they couldn't understand what I had done, could do, or wanted to do with my career, my résumé was ripped apart more times than I could count. While this incessant rework was frustrating, it was a perfect outlet for my perfectionism.

Once my résumés generated frequent favorable responses and positive feedback, I stopped revising them (for the most part). I learned to graciously thank people for their suggestions without feeling compelled to make more changes. I took far longer to get to this place than I would wish for anyone. The final versions of my own résumés received rave reviews from HR/recruiting professionals and hiring managers, and most of my clients landed interviews and jobs with résumés I created.

How Many Résumés Should You Have?

My overall approach to résumés is to create a strong story about what you have done and accomplished, combined with creative, credible, and well-constructed positioning for what you want to do next. It's ideal to have a single résumé that tells your story well, and customize a cover letter for each opportunity.

Others urge job seekers to tweak words (e.g., changing talent management to human capital) to match job postings and increase the odds of getting through Applicant Tracking Systems (Activity 11). Assuming ATS algorithms include a variety of related search terms, I view this as unnecessary.

With my approach, the only exception to having a single résumé is when pursuing two or more distinct career directions. Otherwise, your story can be both compelling and general enough to position you well for many opportunities. I had two résumés that generated exceptional results: one for chief of staff and special assistant to CEO roles; another for writing, editing, and proofreading roles. These directions were distinct enough to warrant a different emphasis when describing my experience and capabilities. The single element I changed was the shaded headline at the top to match the titles of some jobs I applied for (Samples 2-A, 2-B).

Résumés: Most Helpful

Keep it to an appropriate length. Two pages are optimal for a standard business résumé that covers up to 30 years of experience. Academic and other specialized Curricula Vitae (CVs) can easily warrant more than two pages. One-page résumés with education at the top are common for recent college graduates with little professional experience.

Use precise formatting. If you are not adept at formatting, it's worth paying someone to produce a polished document. Whenever possible, submit a PDF instead of a Microsoft Word document to preserve formatting across different software platforms. Submitting PDFs is essential for résumés created in anything other than Word.

Pay attention to white space. Optimize top, bottom, and side margins and other white space. Manage where pages break and include your name on the top of page two.

Choose an appropriate font. Replace Times New Roman with more modern, mostly sans serif fonts (e.g., Arial, Calibri, Candara, Cambria, Tahoma). Eleven-point font size is often best (no smaller than 10-point), but this can vary based on the font and how much information you have. Rather than fancy symbols, use standard bullets embedded in your chosen font for flawless translation across operating systems (usually a non-issue if you submit a PDF).

Leverage the space above the fold (top one-third). Leverage this critical space to stand out from the crowd. Many believe you don't have a chance of being noticed if this top-fold section (created when you fold an 8.5 x 11 piece of paper in thirds) doesn't grab attention.

A common mistake is to write a dense paragraph filled with every overused business term you can think of (e.g., strategic thinker, results-oriented, motivated self-starter, team player, strong communicator, meets or exceeds expectations, proven track record). Don't do it!

I can't overestimate the value of using this section to differentiate yourself. This is your chance to creatively describe the value you bring to an organization. Doing this in an engaging, first-person voice is also gaining popularity. Below are specific ways to maximize the value of this space.

Contact information. Use minimal space (one or two lines) for your contact information by running it across the top under your name. Include hyperlinks for your email address, LinkedIn URL, website(s), and any other online presence suitable for recruiters and hiring managers. List one phone number you monitor closely (usually cell). Include a city and state or geographic region, but not other parts of your mailing address.

Headlines. Synchronize your résumé and LinkedIn headlines. Stand out from the crowd by using creative headlines and sub-headlines that describe the value you bring rather than past or present titles:

- Top headlines should combine keywords that fit multiple targeted positions. Consider customizing this single element of your résumé to include or match titles of jobs you pursue.

- The second line can be a catchy, marketing-oriented tagline or professional branding statement.
- Like your LinkedIn profile, use vertical pipes ("|") to separate elements of your résumé headline(s).

Make a strong case for why employers should hire you:

Top Section. Rather than a traditional "Summary" paragraph, create an exceptionally well-constructed section that demonstrates strengths and accomplishments, and positions you well for what you want to do:

- Mine several advertised jobs you would love to have for key words and phrases to describe yourself. It doesn't matter where they are for this purpose.
- Articulate the essence of what makes you special and the unique value you bring to an organization.
- Instead of *describing* capabilities, *demonstrate* what you've achieved, with as many numerical proof points as possible (show me vs. tell me about it).
- Rather than a dense paragraph, use different formats (e.g., bullets) that are easier to digest.
- Put key words, phrases, and achievements in bold so they stand out.

Skills bank. A common format includes a two- or three-column skills bank. This is losing popularity for non-technical jobs where specific examples of how you've applied these skills are preferred. If you include a skills bank, put it between the top descriptive section and the beginning of your professional experience.

Professional Experience:

- Include all or most of your jobs in reverse chronological order. Include years without months for each job. You might decide to not include your full work history if you are age 50+/- and want to age-proof your résumé.

- Briefly describe your scope of responsibilities and/or the company (no more than three sentences). Put this between the company name and your title(s).

Create strong résumé bullets:

- Emphasize accomplishments, not responsibilities!

- Start each bullet with a strong action verb and vary them across bullets.

- Begin with the impact or *what* you accomplished, followed by *how*.

- Demonstrate (show vs. tell) what you accomplished by including specific examples and results.

- Quantify impact and scope of responsibilities (e.g., revenue, savings, cycle times, volumes, quantities).

- Use current tense for job(s) you're still in; past tense for previous positions.

Select one of two formats to show multiple positions within one company:

Chronological. List each title with its own subset of years and bullets describing what you accomplished in that role. Many executive recruiters require this format.

Hybrid Chronological and Functional. List titles in a reverse chronological order with the subset of years for each. Follow this with several categories of accomplishment bullets that position you well for what you want to do. Use attractive job postings to create these categories. This hybrid format has worked well for all of my résumés.

Include all relevant education and training. List graduate and undergraduate schools, degrees, and honors in reverse chronological order. Don't include years, particularly if you are age 50+/-. Include training and certifications related to your target opportunities. This belongs at the bottom for experienced professionals; at the top for fresh graduates.

Include boards and community involvement. List these in reverse chronological order. Companies with a strong commitment to corporate citizenship view these activities positively.

Exclude "References available upon request." Don't include this obsolete waste of space. Employers assume references are available.

Résumés: Least Helpful

Include a "Search Objective" statement. These are obsolete and should not be included.

Include only 15 years' experience. Heeding this common advice depends on your situation. While including as much of your work history in your résumé that's relevant for your future position(s), limiting your work history in online applications makes sense. (Activity 11: Online Applications and Applicant Tracking Systems).

Your résumé need not tell your whole story. "Less is more" is a popular view. This is based on the premise that the sole purpose for your résumé is to get you invited for an interview. In contrast, my thorough résumés were the most important documents throughout my search. They were the documents of greatest interest to networking contacts, recruiters, and hiring managers. Reasons to leave certain things out (e.g., age proofing) are addressed elsewhere.

Include a summary paragraph in the top one-third. The traditional format for the top summary section is a paragraph. But there is no single right way to design this section and different options are gaining favor. As described in the Most Helpful section above, bullet-like phrases with important words emphasized were well received in my résumés. Use a format that tells your story well, and feel free to stray from a traditional paragraph.

Create a plain text version. Frequent advice is that you must upload a plain text résumé in online applications. I never created a plain text version and had no problems uploading (or cutting and pasting) Microsoft Word and PDF formats.

Create a professional bio. Instead of introducing yourself with your résumé or networking profile, many suggest using a one-page bio, hoping the person subsequently requests your résumé. Like an author or speaker profile, this bio would be written in third person and include a photo. I created a few versions, but never found them to be a useful alternative to my other documents.

Activity 10
Cover Letters

Views differ about the importance of cover letters. Some hiring decision-makers never read them; others won't consider a résumé that arrives without a letter. As noted previously, cover letters could become extinct as one-click online and mobile job applications become more prevalent.

It's sometimes hard to tell whether a traditional online application allows you to attach a letter with your résumé. Sometimes you won't know if you need one until the end of the application, which is not the time to stop and write one. Doing so might get you kicked out of the system for taking too much time. If you're not too frustrated to continue, you might have to start over.

Although writing customized cover letters was the most time-consuming task, my bias was to always include one. And, it was best to write the letter before starting the application (Samples 3-A, 3-B). Keep reading to find out how to submit a letter if you are limited to uploading one document.

 **Cover Letters: Jury's Out**

Address a specific person. Common advice is to address your letter to the recruiter, HR contact, or, better yet, the hiring manger. When job postings followed the typical practice of not naming a specific contact person, I used LinkedIn to find the likely hiring manager or a senior HR/recruiting professional.

After submitting applications through official channels, I often leveraged LinkedIn and the company website to send a copy directly to a higher-level decision-maker or the hiring manager. This worked well sometimes. Other times, it annoyed the HR/recruiting staff members who viewed it as circumventing them. A few asked me to communicate only with them going forward.

 **Cover Letters: Most Helpful**

Use strong subject lines in cover memos and emails. When I couldn't find a specific person to address in a cover letter, I used a memo format. For the subject (RE:), I wrote "Candidate for [Insert Title of Position]."

In email submissions, when I was confident about my strong fit for the job, I used "Strong Candidate for [Insert Title of Position]" as my subject line.

Create standard and customized content. Develop several well-written paragraphs you can reuse or refine for each opportunity. Customize a strong opening and closing, and at least one other paragraph to relate your experience and capabilities directly to the job.

Focus on them vs. you. Focus on what you can do for them, not what they can do for you. Emphasize how you can add value rather than why you want the job. Include one strong sentence in the first and last paragraph about your strong interest in the job.

Manage uploads and attachments. Combine your résumé and cover letter into a single Microsoft Word or PDF document if an online application does not accommodate more than one upload or attachment.

Proceed with caution regarding salary history and requirements. I agree with Liz Ryan's view that your salary *history* is nobody's business. Assertive navigation to discuss only your salary *target* makes a lot of sense (https://www.linkedin.com/pulse/how-answer-what-your-last-salary-liz-ryan).

Many believe it's premature and inappropriate to ask about salary requirements at this early point in the screening process. Others believe it's important to not waste time on further conversations if there's no potential for a compensation match.

While I avoided including salary requirements in cover letters, you could get screened out if the job ad requires this information and you don't include it. Without providing numbers, I acknowledged the question in my last paragraph along these lines: "My salary requirement is flexible and I look forward to discussing this further along in your screening process."

Note: This activity focused on salary requirements in cover letters. Activity 11 focuses on salary requirements in online applications, Activity 22 in interviews, and Activity 25 in negotiating a job offer.

Hold off on providing professional references. Take control of when you provide this information. Common opinions about timing to request and provide references are the same as salary questions. Consistent with the view that this should happen later in the screening process, consider the following options:

- Don't provide contact information for references until necessary.

- If an application requests references, add a sentence in your cover letter when you respond to the salary questions.

For example, "I will be happy to provide professional references at this time."

- For jobs I was most interested in, I included a one-page testimonials document— either with my first submission, in a subsequent correspondence, or during an interview. This was well received and possibly circumvented calls to my references.

Write one-page letters. Keep cover letters to one page and use the same style for your letters and résumé(s) (e.g., fonts, contact information, lines that separate sections).

 Cover Letters: Least Helpful

Use a chart format. A suggested cover letter format included a chart that matched four to six job requirements on the left, with my accomplishments on the right. Letters using this format rather than narrative paragraphs and bullets did not generate responses. I discontinued using charts and would not use them in the future.

Embed complete letters in emails. Some recommend including your whole cover letter in the body of email messages— with or without the letter attached. Finding that many people prefer brief emails, I kept them short and aimed to entice recipients to read my attached cover letter and résumé.

Activity 11
Online Applications and
Applicant Tracking Systems (ATS)

Online applications can be worse than a nuisance (evil). Applicant Tracking Systems are set up to screen out many applicants before their résumés are viewed by human eyes. This unfortunate reality for applicants and employers is due, in part, to too many people applying for jobs that are nowhere close to a good fit.

Even if you can submit your letter and résumé to a specific person, and/or network with someone who can help you get noticed, you probably have to complete an online application at some point. What follows are tips and tricks that did and didn't work for me.

 **Online Applications: Most Helpful**

Apply first, then network. Contrary to common advice, I applied through the company website (or other online channels) first, then worked every angle to gain access to the right people. These actions are based on what worked for me:

- Search LinkedIn for the person likely to be the hiring manager or, at least, someone involved in the hiring decision.

- If you don't have first-degree connections who could introduce you, send a personalized invitation to connect. Send a follow-up email if the person's address is listed, or after he or she (hopefully) accepts your invitation.

- If you can't find the right people on LinkedIn, look on the company website. If you find individuals who might be involved in the hiring decision, approach them through LinkedIn, email, and/or phone (in this order). Some people advise starting with a call. I say good luck getting through gatekeepers, or having the person call you back.

Be the early bird to catch the worm. Apply as soon as possible after jobs are posted. I submitted many applications during the weekend, hoping I would be among the first applicants seen on Monday morning. But don't forget the importance of sending error-free documents!

If not in the first batch, you might get lucky by applying at just the right moment when they are reviewing the pile of applications and deciding who to call.

Don't repeat your résumé. Fill in only as much of the online application as necessary to be considered sufficiently complete. Your goal is to avoid getting screened out by an algorithm and progress to the next step in the process. Cut and paste parts of your résumé when possible, but don't feel compelled to repeat your entire résumé.

- Fill in the most recent 15 to 20 years of professional experience. It must be true, but it need not be your whole story.

- With multiple promotions and titles spanning 20 years in one company, I listed just my last title to cover the entire period. I cut and pasted the short summary description for each job from my résumé with no bullets. I often typed "See Résumé" rather than repeating the whole thing.

- For the ATS screening step, cut and paste or upload your whole résumé in the file format requested. Formatting is irrelevant because the ATS obliterates it and scans for keywords and phrases. It's not necessary to use a plain text version for this purpose.

Choose documents and formats to upload. For coveted human screening steps, upload a PDF or Word version of your résumé and cover letter. As mentioned earlier, if the system accepts only one document, combine them into a single document.

- If an ATS parses information from your résumé into different sections of the application, take time to check and change where different pieces of information land. Make sure your experience is presented exactly the way you want it.

- As discussed in Activity 10: Cover Letters, writing your cover letter before you begin the application will have it ready to attach in the right format at the right time. If you stop to write your letter at the end, you risk getting timed out of the system and having to start over.

- Actively monitor the evolution of cover letter practices.

Navigate salary history and requirement questions carefully. Proceed with caution. Conventional wisdom in salary and other financial negotiations is whoever says the first number loses. As discussed in Activity 10: Cover Letters, many believe salary should not be discussed until an offer is made—when your prospective employer will never love you more. Others believe it should be addressed early, so nobody wastes time if a compensation match is not possible.

As mentioned, leave past, present, and desired salary information blank if the online application allows this. Here are other considerations if answers are required:

- Try entering "Negotiable," zeros, or ranges for your desired/required salary.

- If numbers are required, I like Liz Ryan's suggestion to use your *target* salary to answer *all* salary questions. Attest to your honesty by including a note explaining what you did and your desire to discuss your desired salary (https://www.linkedin.com/pulse/how-answer-what-your-last-salary-liz-ryan).

- If you must submit your current or most recent salary, decide whether including your bonus or variable compensation helps or hurts your chances of getting to the next step.

- Think carefully about how you answer desired/required salary questions. If your salary is negotiable, it can feel like a gamble to go high, medium, or low, relative to your guess about what they want to pay.

I had an uncomfortable situation when I entered my rock-bottom minimum required salary in an online application. My intent was to not get screened out because I was too expensive. I assumed it would be a starting point for negotiations if I received an offer. The employer viewed it as my firm answer for what I wanted to be paid. This led to uncomfortable conversations when I received an offer and negotiated for a base salary higher than I entered in my application.

Addressing this is much simpler if you have and provide a firm salary requirement, making it easier to decide which conversations should progress.

Note: This Activity focused on responding to salary questions in online applications. Activity 10 focused on salary requirements in cover letters, Activity 22 in interviews, and Activity 25 in negotiating a job offer.

Manage your references. Take control of who gets called for a reference, and when. It's ridiculous for employers to ask for contact information as part of the application. Don't provide reference information if the system lets you leave it blank. If required, try to provide just names, titles, and relationships (not email addresses or phone numbers) so you are in control of the reference-checking process. This is explained further in Activity 24: References and Testimonials.

Keep copies. Develop a system to keep track of each application. This can be soft computer files and/or hard paper copies. If you use the same résumé, save just the job posting and your customized cover letter. Besides a pile of hard copies in alphabetical order by company (for easy access when someone called), I created a folder for each company in Microsoft Word and/or Outlook to keep track of all correspondence.

Don't accept rejection emails as a definitive "No." Automated rejection emails can be meaningless. Candidates who receive them often progress through screening steps. Many are generated when an ATS screens out applications and/or résumés based on an algorithm (e.g., too many years' experience or not enough key words). It's not uncommon to receive automated rejection emails and calls from recruiters on the same day. And definitely ignore these rejections if you are networking your way into a company after applying for an advertised position. People you network with won't hesitate to override automated rejections.

Online Applications: Least Helpful

Never apply online. Many career management professionals view online applications as a crapshoot and total waste of time.

They tell job seekers to *never* apply online, and *only* network their way into the company. I say apply first, *then* network into the company.

Pursue long-shot jobs. A common recommendation is to apply for jobs of interest, even if they aren't a strong match with your experience and capabilities. When hundreds of applicants don't take time to seriously consider the role and how they can add value, it lowers the probability for strong candidates to get the attention they deserve.

Activity 12
One-Page Networking Profile
With Target Companies

A networking profile (marketing plan) includes parts of your résumé and a list of target companies. The main purpose for this profile is to ask people you network with introduce you to people in your target companies.

Common advice is to use this profile instead of your résumé in networking calls and meetings, providing your résumé only when requested. Since most people requested my résumé, I sent it before or after a call or meeting, and/or had it with me.

As discussed earlier, identifying target companies can be challenging for Hard-to-Define Professionals. Sweet spot roles are fewer and harder to find. Rather than targeting specific organizations, we need to use broader search parameters to find unusual roles in places we want to work (and avoid places we don't).

Networking Profile: Most Helpful

Generate introductions in target companies. Complement your résumé with a networking profile to communicate what you want to do and request introductions in target organizations.

Focus on single or multiple search strategies. For each interaction, decide whether to use a networking profile to request suggestions and introductions for a single search strategy, or to explore multiple strategies. Each objective could require its own version of the document.

My networking profile was most useful to explore multiple strategies. My résumé was the best document to use when someone could help me with a specific strategy or company. Different types of networking meetings are described in the next activity.

Activity 13
Networking With Purpose:
Quality vs. Quantity of Connections

We've examined the common belief that face-to-face networking is *the* most important activity for job seekers, and dispelled the myth that 80% of jobs are filled as a result of networking. Some people have *always* landed jobs by networking and *never* applied for an advertised job. Others *have* had a job created for them as a result of networking. But I don't believe these successes are prevalent enough for most of us to count on.

So let's look closely at networking with purpose—not just networking—before, during, and after a career transition.

Step Away From Your Computer!

All of these are true: networking often leads to valuable short- and long-term connections, you never know where your next opportunity will come from, and landing a great job can happen through networking. Networking with people you know and meeting new people is extremely important.

But getting out of my pajamas and out of my house to meet with someone (known or unknown) was never first on my list of what I wanted to do. Because I was productive and enjoyed working and writing at home, I tended to isolate myself. Being alone too much could become a debilitating habit. Being out with people was important, energizing, and often sparked new ideas that advanced my writing.

Many job seekers share stories about people and meetings that were more and less helpful than expected. Yep, some meetings I expected to be most helpful were disappointing; others I dragged myself to were most valuable. Case in point was my life-changing experience at the career transition meeting about networking that led me to establish my business (WordsPerfected, LLC).

During my transition, I learned a great deal about how to cultivate meaningful networking relationships. Rather than dreading them, I was surprised by how enjoyable and energizing many meetings were, and how often they led to surprising ways to help each other. You never know who will lead you to someone or something valuable—now, soon, or far into the future.

Even if networking doesn't lead to your next job, it is both critical and rewarding during career transitions—and forever more going forward. Meaningful interactions and relationships continue to evolve with people I met throughout my transition. Some became résumé clients or referral sources. I still enjoy purposeful introductions and interactions within my expanding network. My gradually increasing LinkedIn network is an important and valuable part of my life.

Now that we've confirmed the importance and value of networking, let's further distinguish networking with purpose: aiming for quality vs. quantity of connections and relationships. In contrast to predominant advice to network and connect with as many people as you can, I've always believed that a call or meeting not worth preparing for is not worth having. Good preparation is imperative for networking interactions to be respectful of your contacts' time and productive for you.

Each encounter can be more meaningful and productive when you are selective about who you connect and meet with and why. Thoughtful preparation and diligent follow-through on introductions builds valuable relationships. But a scattershot approach to generating hundreds of connections with less thought and less preparation creates less value for everyone.

People rarely land jobs by networking with strangers at events. However, I enjoy meeting new people and introducing them to someone when I think there's a real possibility for a meaningful connection. I do this sparingly and with clear intention.

I can't overemphasize how important it is to respect the time and attention required to build genuine connections as opposed to going after large numbers (throwing spaghetti against the wall to see what sticks). Effective preparation and follow up means most of us have capacity to develop fewer, deeper connections rather than hundreds that lead nobody anywhere except to burnout. This is particularly true for people who consider themselves introverts.

Several people I heard present on networking topics characterized themselves as strong introverts who had to learn how to network. One speaker boasted about having more than 400 face-to-face meetings in less than a year. He then crashed over the holidays from total exhaustion. He didn't claim significant benefits, and I wondered how much value his odyssey generated for him.

In the realm of job searches, I don't believe über networking is possible to do well, nor is it beneficial to do less well. The further afield introductions and contacts are, without a clear reason for connecting, the less you can understand and help each other. I believed networking more broadly was likely to lead me too far from my sweet spot to be beneficial. This was another departure from most networking advice. Some considered me foolish for declining introductions I thought were too far out of my wheelhouse and likely to point me toward places I had no interest in going.

Clarify Your Purpose for Each Networking Encounter
Networking meetings can serve different purposes. It's important to be clear and selective about your intentions for each interaction. Here are things to think about for different meeting objectives.

1. **Gain access to a specific opportunity or target company.** Be laser-focused to tell a convincing story that sells your strengths, fit, and motivation for that situation. This person might help you rise to the top of the candidate pool for a particular job or gain access to people in a

company of interest (Activity 15: Using LinkedIn to Get Introduced).

2. **Conduct an informational interview.** Talk less; listen more. Learn about a company or possible new career direction. Rather than promoting your value, ask open-ended questions about a company or the person's career progression and landing stories.

3. **Explore multiple search strategies.** Choose carefully with whom you share multiple search strategies for feedback and suggestions. They must be people who can "get it" and help you explore several directions. Others might feel frustrated if they don't understand what you're trying to accomplish and how they can help you achieve a clear objective.

4. **Build relationships.** While remaining selective, expand your network with people who might, at some point, be mutually beneficial. Once you've experienced the enjoyment and value of connecting with purpose, it's important to make this an ongoing part of your life.

 **Networking: Most Helpful**

Be positive, professional, and prepared. Refrain from negative comments about your previous employer(s) and colleagues. Find other avenues for cathartic release and emotional support if you experienced a difficult job loss. Take the time you need to heal and get ready to talk to people with a positive attitude.

As you feel ready to venture out, start with safe family and friends. Avoid high-stakes interactions until your emotions are under control, and you've got your story straight enough to make a good impression on the people most likely to advance your search.

Prepare meticulously. Think carefully about what you want to accomplish in each meeting. Be clear about what you want the person to know about you, and what you want to learn about his or her network and/or career. Create an agenda to bring or send in advance. Sample 5 is an outline you can adapt for different types of networking meetings.

Do your research. Before a meeting, at a minimum, view the person's LinkedIn profile and connections to identify specific requests for introductions. Other sources to learn about people before you meet are Google, company profiles, and résumés. It's also okay to ask them to suggest introductions and target companies.

Make it easy for others to introduce you. Offer to draft an introduction for people to use with their contacts. Most appreciate your making their job easier. Develop reusable content, and thoughtfully tailor these for each introduction. With only so many hours in the day, doing this well is a good reason to emphasize quality over quantity.

Remember that networking is a two-way street. Pay it forward. Everyone tells you networking is more about what you can do for others than what they can do for you. I tried to give at least as much as I got. This was harder when the other person was gainfully employed or retired, and didn't seem to need anything from me.

I always offered to help the other person any way I could at any time. Even if they needed nothing from me then, I never knew what they might contact me about in the future. For example, I received frequent requests and referrals for job search coaching and résumé services from people long after I met them.

Follow up in a timely manner. After each call or meeting, quickly deliver everything you promised with a thoughtful follow-up email or handwritten note. If they offered introductions, follow up as soon as possible—don't let the lead cool down.

Networking Event Etiquette:

Wear your nametag on your right. This puts it in direct line of sight when you shake hands. True confession: I wore mine on the wrong side for many years.

Approach others respectfully. Approach individuals and groups of three or more. Don't interrupt two people because you might intrude on an important conversation.

 **Networking: Least Helpful**

Accept and make unlimited introductions. Be cautious about accepting and requesting introductions from someone who doesn't know you. Also be selective about offering to introduce someone you just met and know nothing about.

One of my worst networking experiences was at a local chapter of a career transition group. Each person presented their one-page profile that included a list of target companies.

The other attendees called out who they could introduce them to at those companies. I was baffled when people offered to introduce someone they just met to someone else they barely knew. On this weak foundation, I wondered why the person receiving the introduction would be willing to spend time with the person being introduced to them. It felt like a meat market and I never went back.

Send an electronic newsletter. Some recommend creating an email newsletter to stay in touch and update your network on your job search progress. The objective is to stay front-of-mind if recipients come across an opportunity that might be a fit for you.

Creating a newsletter was not how I wanted to spend my time or stay in touch with people. Nor would I be interested in reading an update like this from someone in my network. I never created a newsletter, but content suggested by others includes:

- Information of value to your readers, such as a blog post or recommended book
- What happened with your search in recent months
- Companies or people you would like introductions to

If you do this, address privacy matters for your recipients, such as getting permission to include them on your list, including a "safe unsubscribe" feature, or putting all email addresses in "bcc" so people can't see or use them. There are simple email marketing tools (e.g., MailChimp) that automate these details.

Activity 14
Network Tracking Report

While in active networking mode, you need a system to keep track of who you've been in touch with, the nature of the interaction, and when you will follow up. An Excel worksheet was an invaluable tool to manage my networking activities and maintain a pipeline for follow-up and new contacts.

 **Network Tracking Report: Most Helpful**

Manage Last Date/Next Date columns. Actively manage these two most important columns to have a pipeline of people to get in touch with each week—both follow-up and new contacts. At the end of each week, sort the worksheet on the "Next Date" column so the upcoming week's contacts rise to the top. No worries if you need to shift dates and re-sort the worksheet to accommodate your situation for the upcoming week.

Establish a contact database. Use your Tracking Report to manage activity, not to maintain contact information. I tried (unsuccessfully) to create a custom report in Microsoft Outlook that combined my contacts with activity tracking. It was most efficient to maintain my contact database where I had it (in Outlook, syncing with my smartphone and computer), and use this report to track and manage my networking activity.

Optimize your activity level. Sustain networking momentum that pushes you further than you would naturally go, but also fits with your stamina and capacity for preparation and follow-up work. As discussed in Activity 13: Networking With Purpose, each contact requires adequate preparation and follow-up—which takes time.

As I worked harder and longer on my search than some of the most intense times in my jobs, I had to force myself to step away and find balance (no surprise there). Some people procrastinate and get distracted by things they would rather do. While a dedicated, full-time search doesn't guarantee you will land your next job quickly, it will most likely take longer if you don't invest enough time and effort to do the necessary work.

Focus on your priority direction. Devote most of your time and energy to the search strategy you are most interested in. If it's a new direction, it might also be the most intimidating and, therefore, vulnerable to procrastination. If you are serious about making a career shift, you might have to push yourself to go after it.

Keep your pipeline full for setbacks. Don't slow down on job applications and networking in the midst of promising interviews. When you face inevitable disappointments of not getting coveted interviews or job offers, it's important to have other possibilities in play. Avoid periods of not having any balls in the air. Use your support system to help you stay positive and motivated during tough times and dry spells.

 Network Tracking Report: Least Helpful

Set weekly activity goals. Like sales activity management, a common practice is to set goals for the number of calls and meetings to conduct each week (e.g., eight to ten face-to-face meetings). Rather than setting targets, I aimed for what felt like an optimal level of high-quality interactions through multiple methods.

Assign every contact a "Next Date." Some suggest pushing yourself to follow up with people repeatedly and forever. When my connections ran their course, I moved them to the end of my tracking report with "NA" or "TBD" in my "Next Date" column. After months of trying with no response, I concluded I could not get blood out of a stone.

Charge full speed ahead, especially before summer and holiday slowdowns—even if you're falling apart. Despite hitting a wall of depression, I was advised to keep pushing myself to network, especially before the "summer slowdown" set in.

I listened to myself and knew it was time to take a breather. When I couldn't talk to people without crying, it was best to not push myself to network. Having a major setback and suffering from burnout and depression, I had to step back and get help.

It didn't matter that it was April or May, right before the summer months were upon us. In fact, the summer was just as busy, and I landed a job in July. Many fiscal years run July 1 through June 30, so new budget resources can lead to new job requisitions in the summer. Plus, you'll have less competition from other applicants who are on vacation or taking a break.

While the last two weeks of December through the New Year might be the slowest time for recruiting, it doesn't stop completely. When I was home, I continued to find and apply for jobs during these weeks. It was another opportune period with less competition.

Activity 15
Using LinkedIn to Get Introduced

Activity 8 focused on creating your LinkedIn profile and building connections. This section focuses on how to leverage your first- and second-degree connections to:

- Get introduced to someone in a company where you applied for a job

- Introduce yourself to someone who might help where you have applied (e.g., the hiring manager, head of HR, or lead recruiter)

- Meet someone in a target company without a specific opportunity to apply for

 **LinkedIn Introductions: Most Helpful**

Apply first, then network. Contrary to common advice to network your way to interviews *instead* of submitting an application, both are essential. As discussed in Activity 11: Online Applications, *begin* with the standard application process, *then* leverage LinkedIn to network into the company and get your résumé in front of the right people. Whenever I networked with people about a specific advertised job, they advised me to complete the application *and* pursue conversations.

Leverage first- and second-degree connections. When interested in a specific company or job, use LinkedIn to identify people who might help you meet someone or get attention during the screening process:

- Determine if you have first- or second-degree connections who might introduce you to someone involved in a specific hiring decision or area of interest.

- Click on the green link under second-degree connections' photos to see who both of you know.

- Decide if you can leverage your first-degree connection to contact second-degree connections.

- Call or email your first-degree connections, asking for introductions to your second-degree connections who are *their* first-degree connections. Offer to provide a brief paragraph or bullets to help them introduce you.

- Don't hesitate to introduce yourself to someone involved in a hiring decision, or someone you are interested in networking with:
  - Look for a person's personal email address and/or phone number in "Contact Information" under his or her photo, and in the "Advice for Contacting" section near the bottom of the profile.
  - If no direct email or phone number is listed, send a short personalized invitation to connect. Include a request for an email address or to schedule a call. If the person sends his or her email address, follow up with a longer email to request a call or meeting.

- If a direct email address is listed, send a short personalized LinkedIn invitation to connect, and a longer email mentioning you invited them to connect. Ask to schedule a call or meeting in your longer email.

Connect with people who view your profile. Monitor who views your profile and write personalized (*never* boilerplate) invitations to connect with people of interest. For example, "Thanks for viewing my profile. Would you like to connect and have a conversation about XYZ?" These notes are limited to a certain number of characters, so your message must be concise and purposeful.

Activity 16
Recruiters

Recruiters work for and get paid by employers—not candidates. Be wary of anyone who asks you to pay them to place you in a company. External recruiters fit into two categories.

Contingency recruiters get paid when they place people in jobs. They are more likely to work on positions below the highest levels, and less likely to have exclusive searches for client companies. Multiple contingency recruiting firms contacted me for many of the same temporary contracts. It's tricky to navigate which firm presents you for each opportunity and confusing if you are presented by more than one.

Executive recruiters on retainer usually work on higher-level searches and get paid, whether or not they fill a position. They might get paid more once they make a match, and are less likely to have repeat business if they don't.

Since recruiters must fill jobs to get paid or win repeat business, they are most (or only) interested in you if you match a job they are trying to fill. It's hard to get their attention if you don't fit an opening they are trying to fill when you contact them.

 **Recruiters: Most Helpful**

Identify recruiters who specialize in your field(s). Common advice is that it's best to meet them in person. But good luck if you're trying to make this happen without an introduction or a specific search you might help them with.

- A good way to meet recruiters in person is when they speak at professional networking events.

- I had productive calls and meetings with a few recruiters when I was introduced or could mention someone who suggested I call them.

Get in a recruiter's database by means other than sending an unsolicited letter:

- Monitor recruiters' websites and social media updates for active searches. Apply for specific positions to get your résumé into their databases.

- Follow up periodically by phone or email to stay on their radar and let them know you're still looking. Be persistent, but not annoying.

- Build rapport and relationships by referring people to recruiters who call you about opportunities that aren't a fit for you.

 **Recruiters: Least Helpful**

Send unsolicited letters and résumés to a long list of recruiters. This cold campaign is unlikely to yield results—unless your information arrives right when they are looking for someone just like you to fill an active search.

Follow up often to stay on a recruiter's radar screen. Being too persistent will turn them off and land you in their "circular file." This is particularly true when they don't need you, or anyone you know, to fill a position they are working on.

Activity 17
Reasons to Volunteer

Reasons to get involved in volunteer projects before, during, and after a job search:

- Gets you out of your house to interact with people and be involved in something you care about
- Makes a difference related to your personal purpose, passion, or calling
- Provides opportunities to demonstrate your capabilities to people who might be interested or refer you to someone who might be
- Adds community involvement to your résumé and LinkedIn profile—particularly attractive to companies committed to strong corporate citizenship
- Possibly tips a hiring decision in your favor when several top candidates are in the running and your volunteer experience is related to the company, job, or hiring manager

Activity 18
Alternative Work Arrangements:
Contract/Temporary, Part-Time, Freelance

Like volunteer projects, you might have many reasons to do interim work during your transition. Non-traditional work arrangements could also become your new normal.

My résumés listed freelance or consulting projects as my present employment. None of my interviewers skipped a beat when they asked me what I had been doing since leaving my former company.

Finding a variety of interim work became easier when the Affordable Care Act contributed to employers using more contractors and part-time employees to avoid providing health benefits. Technology also made it much easier to find alternative work.

In October 2015, The Freelancers Union released its second annual survey on freelancing in the United States (https://blog. freelancersunion.org/2015/10/01/freelancing-america-2015/). Nearly 54 million Americans (one in three workers) had done freelance work in the past year, and the rising trend was expected to continue.

Reasons to do alternative work:

- Generate income while searching for a full-time job

- Avoid gaps in your résumé and LinkedIn profile

- Add new experiences and capabilities to your repertoire, especially related to your target direction

- Get your foot in the door as a temporary contractor vs. "permanent" employee

- Benefit from companies' increasingly common "try before they buy" practices—allowing employers and employees to ensure a good fit before committing

- Accept contracts that are often extended (sometimes for years) and/or converted into "permanent" jobs

- Gain advantages over external candidates for posted jobs

- Benefit from flexible schedules, opportunities to work remotely, and the option to take breaks between contracts

Ways to find alternative work:

- Register and monitor job postings at temporary staffing companies that focus on jobs in your areas of expertise and interest.

- Register and monitor freelance websites in your areas of expertise and interest. According to the freelancing survey mentioned above, 51% of freelancers found work through online channels. This is sure to increase dramatically over time.

- Volunteer and/or take on small freelance projects you can list on your résumé and LinkedIn profile as your present work. Paid and unpaid work can be listed together as freelance projects. My freelance projects included résumé services, writing and editing projects, market research transcript proofreading, and website testing.

- Create a sole proprietorship or LLC as a consultant or freelancer. Decide if calling yourself the founder, owner, principal, or president is overplaying a one-person entity.

Establish a business and website. This can be a powerful tool to enhance your credibility. Doing so can add a significant boost to your transition story. Any projects or contracts you do during your transition can be listed under this umbrella. Please consult legal and tax professionals before you pursue this option.

Reasons to *not* do alternative work:

- It's challenging to find the time and bandwidth to take on temporary work while doing an intensive full-time job search. You might need to downshift your job search to accommodate a temporary job.

- Income you earn from temporary work must be reported to state unemployment authorities and will be deducted from your compensation during those weeks.

- In my state (Pennsylvania), the minute you promote freelance work or a business entity, you become ineligible for unemployment compensation. This means you can't create a website or business cards, or promote "self-employed" services. Pennsylvania residents are forced to choose between receiving unemployment compensation and trying to build a freelance or small business. There's something wrong with this picture.

- Registering with one or more temporary staffing firms requires time-consuming paperwork that includes personal identification information. I registered with a short list of firms and did not provide complete personal and reference information until they were placing me in a contract.

Working with staffing companies. Staffing company recruiters claim to make better matches than their competitors by more fully understanding the job requirements and more carefully vetting each candidate. One or two recruiters I worked with did this well, but they were the rare exception.

When staffing firm recruiters have commission-based sales quotas, matchmaking can appear superficial. Many seem to focus on filling jobs to get paid rather than ensuring a great fit. This leaves it up to us to ensure the contracts we accept are a good fit.

Activity 19
Updating Your Skills:
New Certifications and/or Courses

Being in transition can be a great time to update or add new skills or certifications to your repertoire. Some state unemployment services offer financial assistance for this. Examples might include project management certifications or courses in software programs or website development.

Activity 20
Personal or Professional Website

Personal websites have become popular. If the content is similar to your résumé and LinkedIn profile, a personal website might demonstrate initiative and creativity to market yourself, but I'm not convinced it's worth the effort. On the other hand, a professional website that promotes freelance services and boosts your credibility is a must if you choose this direction.

You will find a vast selection of free and inexpensive options to build websites, all claiming to be intuitive and user-friendly. Along with creating the website, you must integrate it with a website host, domain name server, custom URL (web address), and email account(s). If the thought of figuring all this out makes you anxious, pay someone to create and configure a website for you. Fitting the pieces together can be overwhelming, and your time might be better spent building the aspects of your business in which you have expertise.

How you design your website depends on how you want it to work for you. At least initially, I did not expect people to find my website through keyword searches. I planned to direct potential clients and employers to the site to build my credibility and provide information about my services. This served its purpose well, and I was not ready to tackle things like search engine optimization (SEO) or Google Analytics.

Activity 21
Social Media and Blogging

Proud of myself for mastering LinkedIn, I had no desire to divert my attention by joining Twitter or Facebook. The latter two platforms had been viewed as more personal and social than professional, but both gained legitimacy for business networking and marketing. Comfort with the mushrooming array of social media platforms is increasingly important as digital natives take over the workforce. People I work with use platforms I've never heard of.

LinkedIn added a platform (Pulse) that made it simple to publish attractive blog posts. Posting and commenting on content has become an essential way to build and promote credible expertise and thought leadership in any discipline. I expect more blogging in my future. And who knows how LinkedIn will evolve after being acquired by Microsoft.

Activity 22
Job Interviews

Congratulations for getting to this point with one or more potential employers! This section addresses both phone and in-person interviews. For as long as you remain interested in an opportunity, your goal in each step of the screening process is to get to the next step. The best way to do this is to be convincing about how you are a great fit for the role.

Most of my initial interviews were by phone. Only one used video (Skype). Some face-to-face interviews were preceded by multiple phone interviews. If you need to use technology you are not familiar with, take time in advance to get comfortable and look professional.

Unfortunately, many phone screens are done by inexperienced internal recruiters who know little about the job, and less about how to learn important things about candidates. Some recruiters use a script and are not permitted to stray from the written questions. It can be frustrating when they are the first screen you must get through before speaking with someone who knows more about the job.

The best phone screens are done by skilled interviewers who understand the company and the job, and know how to learn more about you. Group or panel interviews (by phone and in-person) present special challenges described below.

 **Job Interviews: Most Helpful**

Practice interviewing. Before having to ace interviews that matter, arrange one or more practice interviews with a career coach or HR professional. Videotaping and discussing feedback can be especially valuable. At the very least, practice with a friend or family member who knows something about the hiring process.

Countless books and online resources can help you prepare for typical and difficult interview questions. Practice answering questions you find most difficult.

Prepare thoroughly for phone and in-person interviews. I sometimes put as much time into preparing for a phone screen as a face-to-face interview. The time I spent preparing correlated directly with my level of interest, probable fit for the job, and who was interviewing me.

Hone the parts of your story that demonstrate your strong fit with the company and the job. Whatever they ask, determine three to five concise takeaways you want them to remember about you. Aim to articulate them as the interview starts and ends.

I created and used a template to prepare for each interview (Sample 6). My goal was to understand the organization and the role, position myself as a strong fit, and ask questions that demonstrated my knowledge, insights, and interest.

Learn about your interviewer(s). Ask the person scheduling your interviews for the names and titles of the people who will interview you and how long you will be with each person. Once you know who they are, at a minimum, look them up on LinkedIn. Use your judgment about inviting them to connect before or after the interview (with a personalized note, of course). Common advice was to find information about each person through LinkedIn, the company website, and Google.

Be concise and on-point. While building rapport with the interviewer(s), approach the conversation like being cross-examined by an attorney. Your responses should be concise and not stray from what they're asking. With your goal being to get to the next step, answer the questions, but add nothing extra that could work against you.

Practice behavioral interview questions. Behavioral questions are common and important to answer well. This is where your Accomplishment Stories (Activity 2) come into play. Parts of the stories I had written were specific examples of accomplishments related to the position I was interviewing for. Develop succinct responses that demonstrate the unique value you can bring to the role.

Build rapport with each person during group interviews.
Connect with each person in the group. For in-person panels, make eye contact with each person, even when responding to a question asked by one individual. Group phone interviews were rare and difficult for me. It's impossible to "read the room" and know how they are responding to your answers. I did not get beyond any of these to a next step.

Remain cautious about salary history and requirement questions. Before knowing how to avoid salary *history* conversations, I answered interview questions about my most recent salary with an honest base salary number, and emphasized that my requirements were negotiable.

Common advice was to avoid discussing salary requirement numbers until receiving an offer. One suggestion was to respond to an early question about salary requirements by asking if they are making an offer—too bold for my style. Others believed early salary conversations were essential to determine whether a match was feasible and warranted further consideration.

When asked early, I explained that my salary requirement was flexible in order to find a great fit. For example, "Finding a great fit is most important and my salary requirements are flexible. I would prefer to discuss details further along in the screening process." I avoided providing my target number as long as possible. If you have a firm requirement, you could provide a more definitive answer sooner rather than later.

Note: This activity focused on addressing salary requirements in interviews. Activity 10 focused on addressing salary requirements in cover letters, Activity 11 in online applications, and Activity 25 in negotiating a job offer.

Job Interviews: Least Helpful

Replace phone screens with in-person interviews. Some suggest trying to replace initial phone interviews with in-person meetings. This hard sell didn't work for me. It's difficult to get most employers to stray from their prescribed screening steps. While expecting to follow their process, my goal was to progress to the next step.

Land as many interviews and offers as you can. Many career coaches advise clients to proactively pursue as many interviews and offers as they can. Rather than encouraging and graciously walking away from offers, I followed an approach that fit my needs and values.

Early in my search, when I needed interviewing practice, I accepted a few interviews for jobs I wasn't that excited about. As my search evolved, continuing through screening steps when I knew I would turn down an offer didn't fit my need to be honest and transparent. I became increasingly selective about opportunities I pursued, turned down interviews, and withdrew from consideration when a role was not in my sweet spot.

Activity 23
Follow-Up (Not Thank-You) Notes
After Interviews

Timely follow-up after phone and in-person networking and interviews is one of your most important activities. Whichever method you choose, your follow-up note must be timely, thoughtful, and well written. I put a great deal of thought into my emails and always sent them by the next day—ideally the same day. My

199

follow-up emails were often recognized as key factors in generating additional interviews and job offers (Samples 7A, 7B).

Follow-Up Notes: Most Helpful

Write follow-up vs. thank-you notes. Don't waste your time writing a note that simply thanks people for their time. In addition to more significant content described below, quickly deliver anything you committed to during the conversation.

Make it more about them than you. Focus more on what you can do for them than on what the job can do for you. It's also appropriate to express strong interest in the company and the role. But this is secondary to emphasizing how you can fill their needs or solve their problems.

Emphasize key points regarding your unique fit and value for the role. Maximize the value of follow-up notes as a prime opportunity to reiterate key points about your strong fit for the role, how you can add value, meet their needs, or solve their problems. Repeat the three to five takeaways you identified during interview preparation (Activity 22: Job Interviews).

Follow-Up Notes: Least Helpful

Handwrite and/or mail notes vs. sending emails. Consistent with a common opinion that handwritten notes are rare and more impactful than emails, some people write notes in their cars and hand-deliver them before they leave the parking lot.

Because I put significant time and thought into my follow-up, I always wrote emails after I got home.

Write a separate note to each person. Many coaches advise sending a separate note to each person who interviewed you, plus the administrative staff who assisted you. They recommend responding to each person's questions and reiterating how you can help him or her.

When I had multiple interviewers, they were clearly working as a team to fill the job. This led me to write a single email so they would all receive the same messages without having to compare notes. Sometimes, I addressed specific questions or needs raised by individuals.

Activity 24
References and Testimonials

Like salary questions, asking for and providing contact information for professional references should be left to much later in the process—preferably right before an official offer.

I didn't object to providing names and titles *without* contact information early in a screening process, but I didn't want my references contacted until an offer was pending. It never caused a problem when I responded to written and oral requests by saying I would be happy to provide contact information further along in the process.

 References and Testimonials: Most Helpful

Create a list and ask for agreement. It's never too early in your search to line up a group of people who are ready and willing to serve as professional references when you need them. The next point explains why it might require creativity to develop your list.

Don't rely on colleagues who still work at previous employers for substantive recommendations. Employers have restrictive policies about what information can be provided about former employees. The HR department is generally permitted to confirm dates of service, titles, and, maybe, salary history.

Previous bosses still at the company are usually prohibited from providing qualitative references by phone, in writing on company letterhead, and on LinkedIn. Some might agree to write a letter on personal letterhead. Sharing written letters with potential employers could be useful, but most reference checks are done by phone or email. Other colleagues still at the company are also usually prohibited from providing qualitative feedback (positive or negative) about your skills and performance.

Standard policies make it necessary to get references from people who are no longer at your previous employers. Once they leave, they are free to vouch for you. References are easiest to get, and might be strongest, from people who never were, or are no longer at your most recent company.

Be in control of who calls who and when. Be sure the references you select think you walk on water. Call on different people for different purposes. Save your heavy hitters for reference calls that matter most. Use less significant references (e.g., peers) for opportunities that are less important, such as registrations with temporary staffing firms.

Prepare your references for calls. Prepare your colleagues when you have a live opportunity on the hook and they are likely to be contacted for a reference. Vary the depth of this preparation based on the significance of the opportunity. It could be a short email with brief information about the opportunity, what you would like the reference to confirm about you, and what you told the employer about your relationship with this person. For more significant opportunities, provide more in-depth information about the opportunity and how you positioned yourself as a strong fit.

Secure strong LinkedIn recommendations. One of your earliest action items is to secure at least three to five strong recommendations on LinkedIn. My response to early reference requests was readily accepted when I said: "There are six recommendations from former colleagues on my LinkedIn profile. I am happy to provide contact information further along in your screening process."

Leverage strong LinkedIn recommendations to create a testimonials page or include on your résumé. I capitalized on my LinkedIn recommendations in three ways:

1. **Testimonials page.** I created an attractive page that included my complete LinkedIn recommendations plus a few others. For opportunities I was excited about, I provided this with initial applications or later in the interview process. Potential employers were impressed with the document and it might have caused some to bypass formal reference checks.

2. **Include on résumé (space permitting).** Because I had extra space to play with, page two of my Writer | Editor | Proofreader résumé includes excerpts from recommendations. This was also well received by recruiters.

3. **Include on website.** My website includes excerpts from my LinkedIn recommendations and additional quotes from satisfied clients.

Activity 25
Job Offers and Negotiations

Congratulations—you got a job offer! Now it's your turn to create the best possible overall situation for yourself. If you are at or above director or VP level, you might benefit from professional assistance with your negotiations. Once the terms of your offer are set (see tips below), your employer should send a written agreement that addresses all terms to your satisfaction. Your acceptance of the offer is official when you sign this agreement.

 Job Offers and Negotiations: Most Helpful

Now is the time to ask for everything you want. Your new employer will never love you more than when they make the offer. This is your best chance to negotiate for the full package you want. No guarantees, but things to consider asking for include:

Higher base salary. Having your own market data (e.g., Robert Half Salary Surveys) can help you negotiate a higher salary. I have ended negotiations with numbers higher than original offers.

Higher job level and bonus opportunity. Bonus opportunities generally vary with salary grades, so the higher your salary grade, the better. This might be tough to change from the original offer.

Extra vacation time. If your offer includes less vacation time than you've had or want, this is the time to ask for more. Ideally, the extra time would be paid. You could accept additional unpaid time if the time off is more important than money.

Hiring bonus. These are more common for higher-level positions when an employer wants to sweeten the spot to attract you away from your current position. It's also appropriate to ask your new employer to "make you whole" if they want you to start before you are eligible to receive a year-end bonus at your previous company.

Relocation allowance. These tend to be for higher-level positions, often involving a retained executive recruiter conducting a national search. Specific aspects of such an allowance can be negotiated in your favor.

Health benefit eligibility or cash. If a standard waiting period exists before health benefits kick in, you can ask to have this waived or shortened. If you plan to get your health benefits through another source, you can request a bump in your base salary to make up for the premium you are saving the company.

Title. Think carefully about the job title the company has offered. Ask for any desired change while negotiating the offer. The title on your business cards and soon-to-be updated résumé and LinkedIn profile should position you as you want to be thought of going forward.

Consider how you want your colleagues, customers, and vendors to view you in your new role. Also consider how you might present yourself if you need to move on. Remember, going forward, it's your job to market "Me, Inc.," rather than assume your next position is your last position.

Requests for extra goodies (perks) to sweeten your total compensation deal might include:

Company cell phone or allowance to use your own device. As more companies follow "Bring Your Own Device" (BYOD) practices, allowances are becoming more common than company-owned devices. The nature of your job might dictate whether you warrant having a company-funded device. As I learned the hard way, segregating personal and company information on cell phones is essential, particularly when you move on.

Contribution to your health club membership dues. This is becoming more common as companies add wellness benefits and programs.

Car allowance if you use your own car on the job. This is more common for senior executives and people involved in sales. At a minimum, get reimbursed at the federal rate for any miles you drive while performing your job (excluding your commute).

Golden parachute. While protecting your interests if a separation occurs is probably the last thing you want to think about as you accept a new job, it might be an important step to take. As you climb the corporate ladder, and especially if you relocate, it becomes more important to have a "golden parachute" agreement that sets forth what your new employer would provide if you part ways for any reason. In these cases, it's wise to protect your interests by consulting an attorney with expertise in employment law.

Samples:
Job Searching and Networking Resources

Sample 1
Self-Discovery for
Inventive Career Transitions

10 Questions: What Makes Me Happy?	
1. What am I doing when time flies?	
2. What gives me energy (people, places, activities)?	
3. When am I at my best?	
4. What accomplishments am I most proud of?	
5. What exceptional abilities am I known for?	
6. What do I care about that I would love to integrate with work?	
7. What's my purpose or North Star? What am I most passionate about?	
8. What would I do if I could do anything without concerns about money or failure?	
9. What drains my energy (people, places, activities)?	
10. When do I feel least satisfied with what I'm doing?	

Important Work Factors				
	Very Important	Somewhat Important	Not Important	Avoid
COMPANY OVERVIEW				
Company Size (# Employees)				
Company Size (Financial Measures)				
Publicly Traded				
Privately Held				
Family Owned				
Business Type (Manufacturing / Service / Healthcare / Education / Nonprofit)				
Domestic / International Scope				
Unique Value Proposition (Products / Services / Business Model)				
Socially Responsible / Good Corporate Citizen				
NATURE OF ROLE AND WORK				
Member of Top Leadership Team				
Senior / Middle Manager				
Lead / Manage / Develop staff				
Coach / Mentor Others				
Make Autonomous Decisions				
Strong Guidance From My Leader				
Leader I Trust and Enjoy Working With				
Intellectually Challenging				
Independent Work				
Collaborative Work				
Project Management				
Varied Work				
Fast-Paced / Deadline-Driven				
New Product / Service Development				
P&L Responsibility				
Budgeting / Financial Analysis				
Data / Process Analysis				
Details / Precision				
Sales / Business Development				

NATURE OF ROLE AND WORK (Cont.)	Very Important	Somewhat Important	Not Important	Avoid
Contact With Co-Workers				
Contact With Customers / Clients				
Negotiation				
Public Speaking				
Writing / Editing				
Training / Teaching Others				
Travel (Domestic / International)				
Indoor / Outdoor Work				
Physically Challenging				
COMPANY CULTURE				
Purpose / Mission Fits My Values				
Makes a Difference I Care About				
Focus on Being a Great Place to Work				
Established With Stability and Structure				
Start-Up With Risk, Ambiguity, and Change				
Innovative / Risk-Taking				
Opportunities to Learn, Stretch, and Grow				
Creative People and Environment				
Colleagues I Trust and Enjoy Working With				
Actively Values Diversity and Inclusion				
Attractive Office Location				
TOTAL COMPENSATION AND ADVANCEMENT				
Competitive Base / Bonus Compensation				
Competitive Health Benefits				
Competitive Retirement Plan(s)				
Equity or Opportunity for Ownership				
Clear Career Tracks / Advancement				
Education Reimbursement				
Commute Time / Mode of Transportation				
Ability to Work from Home				
Flexible Schedule				
Relocation with Financial Assistance				

10 Most Important Factors (From Most to Least Important)			
1		6	
2		7	
3		8	
4		9	
5		10	

10 Capabilities / Strengths I Want to Use			
1		6	
2		7	
3		8	
4		9	
5		10	

Take time away before answering these questions. Your thoughts and insights will evolve as you explore and discover what you do and don't want in your next role and environment.

5 "Must Haves" in My Next Work Situation(s)	
1	
2	
3	
4	
5	

5 Things I Want to Avoid in My Next Work Situation(s)	
1	
2	
3	
4	
5	

Sample 2-A
Résumés

NANCY BROUT

Geographic Region	Cell Phone Number	Email Address	LinkedIn Profile

CHIEF OF STAFF | SPECIAL ASSISTANT TO CEO

Writing | Editing | Presentations | Projects | Programs | Planning | Meetings | Events | Constituent Relationships

CATALYST: Causes C-level executives to be more aligned, effective, and efficient. Keeps people and projects connected and moving forward to achieve results. Navigates a course through ideas, frameworks, projects, execution, and results.

TRUSTED PARTNER: Serves as sounding board and advisor to colleagues across levels and sectors. Earns respect and influence through broad business acumen, strong interpersonal skills and relationships, good listening, and objective dialogue. Maintains confidentiality of sensitive information.

MASTER ORGANIZER: Thinks strategically with an eagle eye for tactical details. Leads complex projects from concept to completion. Gets results as an exceptionally organized individual contributor and collaborative team member.

PERSUASIVE COMMUNICATOR: Delivers clear, concise, and compelling messages that inform, engage, and inspire. Clearly articulates abstract ideas, distills insights from complex information, and ensures accuracy of details.

EXECUTIVE LIAISON AND FACILITATOR: Orchestrates committees, teams, and projects with multiple stakeholders.

EXPERIENCE

COMMUNICATIONS PROJECTS   **2014 – Present**
Collaborates with clients to articulate strategies, abstract ideas, and complex information as compelling written copy and presentations. Writes, enhances, edits, and proofreads content to ensure clarity, flow, and technical precision.

FINANCIAL SERVICES COMPANY   **1993 – 2013**
Reported to chairman, president & CEO as trusted partner, catalyst, coordinator, liaison, and facilitator for senior executive team meetings, communications, planning activities, special projects, and consulting engagements. [Add details on company, such as market share, total assets, number of financial professionals.]

AVP, Corporate Planning; Executive Director, Customer Advisory Council	2010 – 2013
AVP, Corporate Planning and Process Excellence	2006 – 2009
Director / Manager / Senior Associate, Corporate Planning	1995 – 2006
Assistant to Chief of Staff	1993 – 1994

Executive Team Liaison and Facilitator

- Partnered with C-level executives and teams to align and advance strategy, execution, and results by setting strategic priorities, leading special projects, monitoring progress, and meeting critical deadlines.
- Impacted company performance by staffing enterprise engagements with more than 10 consulting firms.
- Orchestrated company-wide, town hall, advisory council, and weekly executive team meetings to identify and achieve outcome objectives through effective agendas, materials, minutes, action item tracking, and logistics.
- Optimized day-to-day corporate office operations, communications, and complex calendar management as staff liaison among the executive office, department heads, and executive/administrative assistants.

Internal and External Communications

- Researched, wrote, edited, and managed production of high-impact executive communications; partnered on sensitive messaging with corporate communications, human resources, and legal.
  - Audiences included boards, executives, leaders, associates, clients, industry conferences, ratings analysts.
  - Vehicles included executive PowerPoint presentations, speeches, talking points, and correspondence; web content, videos, newsletters, and promotional flyers.
- Positioned company strategy and performance for best possible ratings by leading complex annual process to analyze rating agency perspectives, develop PowerPoint decks, and prepare executives for presentations.
  - Helped company earn upgrades and sustain ratings through challenging period of economic turmoil by leading executives through process to strategize, prepare, and deliver briefings.
  - Wrote, edited, and produced "Best Practice" presentation and fact book materials in partnership with CFO.
- Drove decisions, actions, results, and learning by synthesizing complex information into incisive PowerPoint presentations, meeting notes, project plans, tracking reports, and "lessons learned" debriefs.

Special Projects and Programs

- Increased strategic alignment by facilitating company-wide process to develop vision, mission, and values.
- Contributed to best-in-class voluntary turnover rates below 5%, and employee engagement survey scores well above industry benchmarks, by pioneering corporate culture and employee engagement initiatives.
- Managed complex financial transaction ($200M surplus notes) and creation of extensive due diligence library; project team of 50+ members included multiple external investment banking and law firms.
- Developed first reports for state insurance departments on compliance with sales practice regulations.

Constituent Relationships: Customer Advisory Board and Committees

- Contributed to 66% increase in active distributor (customer) population and 82% growth in sales by leading a customer advisory council that significantly increased market intelligence, loyalty, and sales.
- Strengthened advisory board and committees as a powerful conduit for ongoing customer feedback and market intelligence via promotional communications that significantly increased awareness, participation, and value.
- Enabled company to design and deliver more competitive products and services to financial professionals and their clients by restructuring, training, and consulting to committees that leveraged customer feedback.
  - Provided broader range of customer perspectives by recruiting 10 new board members in two years.
  - Engaged more than 180 individuals on 13 active committees through virtual and live meetings.
  - Achieved higher sales and satisfaction from products and services tested and refined with customers.

Strategic and Operational Planning

- Contributed to above-industry profitable and sustainable growth by helping executive team align and integrate strategy, financial goals, and operations by coordinating planning, budgeting, and reporting cycles.
- Facilitated development of five-year strategic plan with chairman and consultants; approved by board.
- Planned and conducted strategic and operational planning retreats as partner to executives and consultants.
- Designed and delivered, in collaboration with PwC consulting partners, two-day competitive scenario planning retreat for executives and extended leadership team of 24 participants.

GREATER PHILADELPHIA CHAMBER OF COMMERCE   **1986 – 1993**
Philadelphia Area Council for Excellence (PACE)
Directed training and consulting services on process improvement via Total Quality Management (TQM) for C-level executives in manufacturing, service, government, healthcare, and academia. Featured Dr. W. Edwards Deming, Tom Peters, and other internationally renowned thought leaders. Managed $1.3 million budget, advisory board, and daily operations of 9-person department. PACE was most profitable program of 8th largest Chamber of Commerce.

     Director   1990 – 1993
     Assistant Director   1986 – 1990

- Led development, marketing, and delivery of 25 annual training programs attended by 3,500 senior executives.
- Researched, wrote, edited, and managed production of catalogs, brochures, newsletters, print, and radio ads; authored proposals, plan documents, presentations, correspondence, and meeting minutes.
- Established Greater Philadelphia Healthcare Network for 27 hospitals implementing Continuous Quality Improvement (CQI) to meet Joint Commission accreditation requirements.
- Generated substantial revenue by recruiting 60 corporate and 400 individual members by marketing valuable membership benefits.
- Met client needs through design and delivery of customized training programs and consulting services.
- Presented on TQM concepts and Council activities; consulted to start-up Excellence Centers across the U.S.

ALDERSGATE YOUTH SERVICE BUREAU   **1982 – 1985**
Created and delivered state-funded drug and alcohol prevention programs and services to public school students in Eastern Montgomery County, PA. Provided individual, group, and family counseling; facilitated Parent Effectiveness Training for 200 parents. Aldersgate is a nonprofit social service agency for children and families.

     Drug & Alcohol Prevention Specialist; Individual, Group & Family Counselor

- Proposed, created, and presented programs for 5,000 educators, parents, and students in grades K-8.
- Prepared state funding and board reports; maintained program records and billing statistics.
- Researched, developed, and taught Temple University undergraduate course on drug and alcohol issues.

EDUCATION

M.S.Ed., University of Pennsylvania, Psychological Services/Counseling Psychology
B.A., Clark University, Psychology and Sociology

Sample 2-B
Résumés

NANCY BROUT

| Geographic Region | LinkedIn Profile | Website Link | Email Address | Cell Phone Number |

WRITER | EDITOR | PROOFREADER | PRESENTATION SPECIALIST
Ideas, words, grammar, and format perfected!

Meticulous wordsmith perfects messaging, style, composition, grammar, punctuation, and format. Writes, edits, and proofreads content to ensure clarity, flow, and technical precision. Thinks strategically to find the right words to inform, engage, and inspire audiences. Fine tunes copy, data, and format with an eagle eye for accuracy and ability to focus on details for long periods. Exceptionally organized individual contributor, and collaborative and influential team member. Brings corporate and nonprofit experience, with knowledge of financial and investment concepts, products, and services.

- Partners with C-level clients, marketing, and SMEs to develop clear content with strong brand consistency.
- Collaborates with creative team members on concepts, design, and layout for print and PowerPoint presentations.
- Edits and proofreads for flawless grammar and accurate changes in each stage of editorial process.
- Coordinates precise and timely reviews, revisions, and approvals to meet production schedules.
- Manages projects and production to meet tight deadlines and budgets.

Audiences	Content	Documents	Technical Skills
• Boards; Committees	• PowerPoint Decks	• Word
• Executives	• Strategic and Operating Plans	• PowerPoint
• Employees/Associates	• Annual Reports; Proposals	• Excel
• Clients/Customers; Distributors	• Web Content; Videos; Newsletters	• Outlook; Lotus Notes
• Rating Agency Financial	• Marketing Catalogs; Brochures; Flyers	• Adobe Acrobat
Analysts	• Speeches; Speaking Points; Correspondence	• AP Stylebook
• Industry Conference Attendees	• Market Research Transcripts and Surveys	• Transcription

EXPERIENCE

FREELANCE WRITER, EDITOR, PROOFREADER   2014 – Present
Collaborates with clients to articulate strategies, abstract ideas, and complex information as compelling copy and presentations. Writes, enhances, edits, and proofreads content to ensure clarity, flow, and technical precision.

Sample Projects:
- HR Communications Editor (Contractor)
- Strategic Plan PowerPoint Presentation for Nonprofit Board
- Leadership Coaching Manual; Leader and Program Coordinator Guide for Online Course
- Resumes and Cover Letters; LinkedIn Profiles

FINANCIAL SERVICES COMPANY   1993 – 2013
Reporting to chairman and SVP of marketing, wrote, edited and/or proofread internal and external communications. Collaborated on strategic and sensitive messaging with C-level executives, marketing, communications, HR, and legal. Coordinated design and production with creative staff and print vendors. [Add details on company.]

Marketing & Communications; Customer Advisory Council 2011 – 2013
Executive Office: Corporate Planning and Process Excellence 1993 – 2010

Sample Writing, Editing, and Proofreading Projects:
- Annual PowerPoint presentation and fact book considered "Best Practice" quality by rating agency financial analysts; partnered with CFO to tell the story behind the numbers and prepare executives for presentations.
- Strategic and operating plan booklets and PowerPoint decks presented to board and all employees.
- CEO PowerPoint presentations, reports, and minutes for board of trustees.
- Company meetings and executive communications that contributed to strategic alignment, employee engagement survey scores well above industry benchmarks, and best-in-class voluntary turnover < 5%.
- Quarterly newsletters, video scripts, web content, and speeches to promote customer advisory board and committees; managed 15 monthly conference calls and two annual meetings w/progress reports and minutes.
- Annual reports, marketing brochures, quarterly employee newsletters, and health plan open enrollment materials.
- Market research and employee engagement survey questions; edited and categorized open-ended responses to identify themes and facilitate action planning.
- Meeting notes, project plans, tracking reports, and "lessons learned" debriefs that facilitated decisions and actions.
- PowerPoint templates and style guides that drove consistency across presentations.

GREATER PHILADELPHIA CHAMBER OF COMMERCE   1986 – 1993
Philadelphia Area Council for Excellence (PACE)

Directed training and consulting services on process improvement via Total Quality Management (TQM) for C-level executives in manufacturing, service, government, healthcare, and academia. Featured Dr. W. Edwards Deming, Tom Peters, and other thought leaders. PACE was most profitable program of 8th largest chamber of commerce.

Director   1990 – 1993
Assistant Director   1986 – 1990

- Led development, marketing, and delivery of 25 annual training programs attended by 3,500 senior executives.
- Researched, wrote, edited, proofread, and managed production of catalogs, brochures, newsletters, print, and radio ads; authored proposals, plan documents, presentations, correspondence, and board meeting minutes.
- Generated substantial revenue by recruiting 60 corporate and 400 individual members by marketing valuable membership benefits.
- Established Greater Philadelphia Healthcare Network for 27 hospitals implementing Continuous Quality Improvement (CQI) to meet Joint Commission accreditation requirements.

EDUCATION

M.S.Ed., University of Pennsylvania, Psychological Services/Counseling Psychology
B.A., Clark University, Psychology and Sociology

TESTIMONIALS

"I often relied on her exceptionally strong writing and editing abilities for internal and external audiences. I highly recommend Nancy, without reservation, for any professional opportunities she pursues."

Chairman & CEO (Retired)

"Her exceptional capabilities include executive level coaching and facilitation, writing and editing, project management and organization."

Chief Financial Officer (Retired)

"She had excellent project management, facilitation, and problem solving skills, as well as meticulous attention to detail. She utilized superior and creative writing and editing abilities to create strong marketing and promotional pieces, executive presentations, and grant proposals."

Group Vice President (Retired)

"Nancy has exceptional administrative skills and she can take the most complex projects and give them a clarity which anyone can understand."

President, Customer Advisory Council (2013 – 2014)

Sample 3-A
Cover Letters

NANCY BROUT

Email address   Cell: xxx.xxx.xxxx

Date

Ms. [Insert First and Last Name]
Title
Company
Address 1
Address 2

Dear Ms. [Insert Last Name],

As a trusted partner to the Chairman and CEO (retired) of [Company], I am a strong candidate for your **Special Assistant** position. In addition to helping senior executives, advisory boards, and committees be more effective and efficient, I help them align and advance strategic priorities, communications, special projects, and constituent relationships. This position is exactly the type of staff assistant role I am seeking in a mission- and values-driven organization.

My experience in corporate and nonprofit organizations would enable me to bring distinct value to this unique position. Creating clear and compelling executive communications and PowerPoint presentations for internal and external audiences has been a career focus. I have been a high-level administrator and advisor to corporate and nonprofit boards, committees, and projects that involved multiple constituents. Administrative colleagues often sought and appreciated my guidance as a trusted mentor.

I would like to highlight additional areas of expertise directly related to this position:

- Writing, editing, and production of executive correspondence, PowerPoint presentations, speeches, and speaking points
- Analysis and presentation of financial and other data in Excel spreadsheets and PowerPoint presentations
- A-to-Z orchestration of a wide range of senior management, advisory board, committee, and company meetings and special events (agenda planning, preparation of presentations and speakers, participant materials, facilitation, and logistics)
- Grant-related documents and data reporting
- Oversight and coordination of executive and organization-wide calendars and annual events
- Complete confidentiality when dealing with sensitive information

It would be an honor to work with the senior management team and board of a premier educational institution dedicated to developing accomplished leaders. I have enclosed testimonials from colleagues and will be happy to provide contact information further along in your screening process. I look forward to speaking with you to explore the significant contributions I can bring to [Organization]. Thank you for your consideration.

Sincerely,

Nancy Brout
Nancy Brout

Sample 3-B
Cover Letters

NANCY BROUT

Email address   Cell: xxx.xxx.xxxx

TO: [Company and Department Name or Human Resources]

FROM: [Your Name]

RE: **EDITOR/WRITER: CORPORATE MARKETING**

DATE: [Insert]

I am a skilled writer, editor, and proofreader with over 20 years' experience in financial services. As a meticulous wordsmith, I am passionate about using language to create shared meaning and drive results. In addition to writing, I perfect content others have drafted or envisioned. I do this with strategic insights and an eagle eye for details.

Creating clear, concise, and compelling content has been a career focus. From my role within the executive office, I partnered with corporate communications, marketing, human resources, and legal to develop consistent messaging for multiple audiences. During the last three years, I became part of the Strategic Marketing, Planning, and Communications team. Throughout my tenure, I was involved in synchronizing a broad range of communications with the company's strategy and brand.

At [Company], I collaborated with executives and actuaries as the lead writer, editor, and project manager for annual executive briefings to rating agency analysts. I worked closely with the chief financial and investment officers to tell the story behind the numbers. I was also the internal project manager for a $200 million surplus note transaction. These projects provided broad exposure to complex financial and investment concepts. I have managed many communications projects through all phases. This included research, writing, editing, design, and production of printed documents, PowerPoint presentations, speeches and speaking points, articles, videos, and web content.

I enjoy collaborating and managing action items to complete superior quality work products within expected timeframes and budgets. I approach all of my work with a passion for ongoing learning and process improvement to deliver the highest quality in the most efficient manner. Broad business acumen and strong interpersonal skills enable me to work with diverse stakeholders and add value to a wide range of opportunities and challenges.

I look forward to conversations about the significant contributions I can bring to [Company's] corporate marketing team. Thank you for your consideration.

Sample 4
One-Page Networking Profile
With Target Companies

NANCY BROUT

Email address	Cell Phone Number	LinkedIn Profile

INTERNAL SERVICES ROLE IN MANAGEMENT CONSULTING
OR
CHIEF OF STAFF | SPECIAL ASSISTANT TO CEO

Writing | Editing | Presentations | Projects | Programs | Planning | Meetings | Events | Constituent Relationships

CATALYST: Causes C-level executives to be more aligned, effective, and efficient. Keeps people and projects connected and moving forward to achieve results. Navigates a course through ideas, frameworks, projects, execution, and results.

TRUSTED PARTNER: Serves as sounding board and advisor to colleagues across levels and sectors. Earns respect and influence through broad business acumen, strong interpersonal skills and relationships, good listening, and objective dialogue. Maintains confidentiality of sensitive information.

MASTER ORGANIZER: Thinks strategically with an eagle eye for tactical details. Leads complex projects from concept to completion. Gets results as an exceptionally organized individual contributor and collaborative team member.

PERSUASIVE COMMUNICATOR: Delivers clear, concise, and compelling messages that inform, engage, and inspire. Clearly articulates abstract ideas, distills insights from complex information, and ensures accuracy of details.

EXECUTIVE LIAISON AND FACILITATOR: Orchestrates committees, teams, and projects with multiple stakeholders.

PROFESSIONAL EXPERIENCE

Communications & Consulting Projects	2014 – Present
Financial Services Company	1993 – 2013
AVP, Corporate Planning; Executive Director, Customer Advisory Council	2010 – 2013
AVP, Corporate Planning and Process Excellence	2006 – 2009
Director / Manager / Associate, Corporate Planning	1995 – 2006
Assistant to Chief of Staff	1993 – 1994
Greater Philadelphia Chamber of Commerce, Philadelphia Area Council For Excellence (PACE)	1986 – 1993
Director / Assistant Director	
Aldersgate Youth Service Bureau	1982 – 1985
Drug and Alcohol Prevention Specialist; Individual, Group, and Family Counselor	

SAMPLE DELAWARE VALLEY TARGET ORGANIZATIONS (As of xx/xx/xx)

Management Consulting Professional Services	Nonprofits Universities / Exec. Ed. / Health Care	Corporate
Small/Mid-Size Firms	**Non-Profits**	**Financial Services**
Ballentree Consulting / CEO ThinkTank	ABIM - American Board of Internal Medicine	ACE Group
DSI - Decision Strategies International	CED – Community Economic Development	Chatham Financial
Gap International	CDP - Cultural Data Project	Cigna
Navigate Corporation	NBME – National Board of Medical Examiners	Citadel FCU
RHR International	Pew Charitable Trust	Credit Suisse, Private Banking NA
Richardson Group	PMI – Project Management Institute	Hartford Funds
The Conference Board	TRF - The Reinvestment Fund	JP Morgan
UpStreme	WORC - Women's Opp. Resource Center	Lincoln Financial Group
Large Firms	**Universities / Executive Education**	Sallie Mae
Deloitte Consulting	Bryn Mawr / Haverford	Vanguard
PwC	Drexel	Vizant
Accenture; EY	Penn State Great Valley	
GP Strategies / Blessing White	Princeton	**Other Industries**
Grant Thornton	University of Pennsylvania / Wharton	Accolade
Morgan, Lewis & Bockius	Ursinus College	Axalta Coating Systems
Navigant Consulting, Inc.	Villanova	Endo Pharmaceuticals
North Highland	West Chester University	GreenPhire
Hay Group	**Hospitals / Health Care**	SAP
Korn Ferry	Jefferson	TMG Health
LHH	Main Line Health	
Right Mgt.	TMG Health	
Towers Watson	Wills Eye Hospital	

EDUCATION: M.S.Ed. Psychological Services/Counseling Psychology, University of Pennsylvania
             B.A.   Psychology and Sociology, Clark University

Sample 5
Preparation for Networking Meetings

Contact Profile and Questions

- Name
- Title
- Company / Organization
- Tenure
- How Met / Introduced
- Shared LinkedIn Connections
- Previous Employers

My Story and Requests

- My Goals for Meeting
- My Career Progression
- My Special Focus Areas
- My Search Objectives
- My Target Companies
- How Can This Person Help Me?
  - Intros or Use their Name to Meet Their First-Degree Connections (Offer to Draft for Them)
- Their Advice/Suggestions
  - My Search
  - My Résumé
  - My Target Companies
- What Can I do for Them?

Additional Questions for Informational Interviews

- Previous Roles / Focus Areas
- Tenure in Roles
- Career Progression
- How They Got Their Jobs
- Current Responsibilities / Key Focus Areas
- Education
- Special Training / Certifications
- Advice to Help Me Enter This Field

Sample 6
Preparation for Interviews

Company Name:
Job Title:
Interviewers: Names, Titles, Tenure, Special Notes

Elevator Pitch: 3 Key Messages to Respond to "Tell me/us about yourself." (whether or not they ask)

Why Do They Need Me: Why Am I a Great Fit for This Role / My Unique Value for Them?

Why Do I Want This Job: Why Do I Want to Work Here / This Job?

Things I Should Know: Company / Industry

Common Interview Questions

- Why did you leave your last position?
- Why do you want this job?
- Why you? What are your strongest capabilities for this job?
- Examples of how you accomplished key aspects of the job
- Areas for development / feedback received
- Example of a mistake you made: what happened; how did you fix it; what did you learn; how did you prevent a recurrence?
- How do you deal with multiple competing priorities?
- How do you stay organized?

- Do you prefer a micro-manager or inaccessible boss?
- Five-year vision / goals for yourself?
- What are your non-work activities / interests / passions?

Sample Questions to Ask Interviewers

- Why is the position open (e.g., new position, internal promotion, lateral move, left company)?
- Focus areas / priorities for the position / key gaps or needs to fill
- Key working relationships for role (internal / external)
- Key challenges to succeed in role
- Expectations / metrics for success (3, 6, 12 months)
- Describe the culture / best aspects of working here
- What is the tenure / turnover in the department? Company?
- Next Steps / Additional Interviews
  - Target Timing for Decision/Offer
  - Target Start Date

Position Description Chart

Prepare a strong case for why you are a great fit for the role. This will help you answer behavioral interview questions by demonstrating accomplishments directly related to the job. Do this by creating a two-column chart with key job requirements on the left and your key accomplishments that match each requirement on the right.

Sample 7-A
Follow-Up (Not Thank-You) Notes
After Interviews

Background

Email sent after in-person interviews at Gap International where I landed my business writer and editor position. Although I met individually with two hiring managers, I sent this email to both. In addition to reiterating my fit for the role, I added information I forgot to mention in the interview.

Dear [First Name] and [First Name],

I'm so glad we were able to meet before I begin my three-month contract at [Company Name]. It was great to learn more about how Gap International's work is evolving. Our conversations strengthened many favorable impressions that have captured my interest over the past year.

We are all in an enviable position to afford being highly selective in our choices. I am excited about your interest in the rare combination of professional experiences and capabilities I can bring to the business writer role. Among these are my corporate C-suite experience and business acumen, passion for using words and images that create shared meaning and drive outcomes, and deep respect for the powerful magic of true ("full contact") collaboration.

I forgot to mention something important to [Name]. After [Company Name's] chairman and CEO retired, I joined the Marketing & Communications team. One of my accomplishments was to develop a full-year marketing and communications calendar that captured all key campaigns and events that were scheduled.

Gap International is clearly a unique company to join. I came away from today thinking we would enjoy working together, and looking forward to continuing our conversations. Meanwhile, I wish you both a wonderful Thanksgiving.

Regards,

Sample 7-B
Follow-Up (Not Thank-You) Notes
After Interviews

Background

Email sent after separate in-person interviews with a hiring manager and the person leaving a full-time temporary contract I was interviewing for. I received and declined an offer because it was early in my search and I had a few other opportunities in progress. This was just before I accepted the three-month editing contract that was a stronger fit with my interests.

Hello [First Name] and [First Name],

Thank you for your time yesterday. I came away with a good overview of your PowerPoint and project coordination needs. I am confident I can step in to deliver a high-quality weekly deck. I can also help [Name's] team fulfill requests for new information from those who rely on your reports.

It's clear that [Name] has done a great job for the team, so I recognize she has big shoes to fill. Providing this support for [Company's] global cloud DC projects is a great opportunity to add value and learn about an exciting business. I look forward to speaking with [Staffing Recruiter's Name] as you make your decision.

Regards,

ARTIST STATEMENT

FREEDOM

Sculptor: Zenos Frudakis
Date of Dedication: June 18, 2001
Location: 16th & Vine, Philadelphia, PA

My Discovery of *Freedom*

My mother sent me an email with photographs of sculptures from around the world. The moment I saw *Freedom*, I knew it belonged on the cover of this book as a profound representation of the despair, recovery, discovery, and triumph I experienced.

Thrilled to discover that *Freedom* is in Philadelphia (my city), I received a warm and gracious "Yes!" in response to an email describing my book and requesting permission to feature the sculpture on the cover. Along with the privilege of meeting Zenos and Rosalie Frudakis and touring his studio, Zenos granted permission to include his complete artist statement as it appears on http://www.zenosfrudakis.com.

I wanted to create a sculpture almost anyone, regardless of their background, could look at and instantly recognize that it is about the idea of struggling to break free. This sculpture is about the struggle for achievement of freedom through the creative process.

– ZENOS FRUDAKIS

Complete Artist Statement

Although for me, this feeling sprang from a particular personal situation, I was conscious that it was a universal desire with almost everyone; that need to escape from some situation—be it an internal struggle or an adversarial circumstance, and to be free from it.

I began this work in a very traditional sculptural manner by creating a small model in clay called a macquette. The purpose of beginning in this manner is to capture the large action and major proportions of the figure within the overall design without any details to detract from the big idea. Another reason for not having details and for working on a small model only a few inches in height is that the small armature within it, holding the clay, is more easily manipulated, allowing for much greater flexibility in developing a concept. For example, an arm, a leg or a head can be pushed around without any concern for obliterating details, such as a nose or a finger.

The macquette is the original mass of clay where a concept is born and from which it grows and develops. This was important later when I enlarged the sculpture from several inches long to 20 feet long, and I retained in the larger work a sense that all the conceptual material, its forms, focus and development sprang from this rough idea. The work metamorphosized, in the way that we do.

Although there are four figures represented, the work is really one figure moving from left to right. The composition develops from left to right beginning with a kind of mummy/death like captive figure locked into its background. In the second frame, the figure, reminiscent of Michelangelo's **Rebellious Slave**, begins to stir and struggle to escape. The figure in the third frame has torn himself from the wall that held him captive and is stepping out, reaching for freedom. In the fourth frame, the figure is entirely free, victorious, arms outstretched, completely away from the wall and from the grave space he left behind. He evokes an escape from his own mortality.

In working on the large-scale sculpture, I was satisfied that those who drove by getting a quick look at it would see the big picture: that it was about escape. I was also concerned that those who worked in the building and who passed the sculpture frequently would have something more to see. There was a lot of empty space between the figures on the wall, which I saw as an opportunity to develop further ideas.

It was important to me that the sculpture have more than one theme going on at once. One of the other major ideas incorporated in the work is that the very process of creating the sculpture is clearly revealed in the work itself. The macquette is cast into the sculpture in the lower left hand corner. In the lower right corner is the cast of the sculptor's hand holding the sculpture tool with two rolls of clay also cast in bronze. Throughout the background of the Wall, I have rolled out the clay and pressed it with my fingers so that my fingerprints are all over the sculpture. I have not hidden how I have made the piece. In fact, the whole idea of the macquette is enlarged so that all the figures in the background look like a giant macquette. And at the same time, as the figures move from left to right, I have shown how figures are developed when you are sculpting from the rough to the more finished product.

Elements of the sculpture trade beside the tools that are cast into the sculpture are calipers both for their use in measuring and their reference to Protagoras' words "*Man is the measure of all things.*"

Also cast into the sculpture is an anatomical man, tradition-ally used as a reference by sculptors. Many of the heads and figures on the wall, some in the round and some in relief, are shown partially sculpted, revealing the process of creation.

Something else I have done with the sculpture is that I have created a one man show of my work. I have always admired Rodin's **Gates of Hell**. I similarly thought I would incorporate many sculptures into the wall where it was suitable.

Like T.S. Eliot and other artists, I have put many personal elements in my work. My friend Philip, a sculptor who died of AIDS, created a work that I included in Freedom because he often expressed his wish to have it in a public space. He did not live long enough to accomplish this himself. My cat, who lived with me for 20 years, my mother, father, and my self-portrait are in the work. It is obvious which face is mine because there is a ballooned phrase coming from my mouth with the word "freedom," written backwards, making it clear that the face was sculpted in a mirror. I see the whole Wall sculpture as a kind of illusion akin to Alice's **Through the Looking Glass.**

The sculpture contains an original Duane Hanson—a bronze cast of my own hands that Duane cast for me as a gift.

Much of what I did with this sculpture has to do with taking traditional forms and combining them in non-traditional ways, forming a postmodern sensibility. For example, I dropped a wax cast of my father's bust from two or three feet in height so that it broke into large pieces. I cast those into the wall in a fractured manner over another face, an old work I found in a vat of clay purchased from a sculptor who had long ago died.

I have hidden many things in the background for people who see the sculpture more than once to discover, such as a cast of coins—a nickel and two pennies, another nickel and two pennies, and two quarters and a penny. These represent not only the relationship between money and art, but the numerals 7-7-51, my birth date.

It is important to me that the public interact with the sculpture, not just intellectually and emotionally but physically. I have created a space in which I have written **"stand here"** so that people can place themselves inside the sculpture and become part of the composition.

In the end, this sculpture is a statement about the artist's attempt to free himself from the constraints of mortality through a long lasting creative form.

ACKNOWLEDGEMENTS

My memoir includes a *Silver Linings List,* but my transformation and this book have a precious platinum lining. My tribe of special people grew wider and deeper as I struggled, triumphed, and created this book. I am eternally grateful to each person who played a role as I found myself and invented my next chapter.

The most cherished member of my tribe was and is Bryan Hutchinson, my loving husband. He stood by me through good days and many bad ones, never knowing "which wife" he would encounter when he walked in the door. Fortunately, our lives usually follow a seesaw pattern, with one of us up while the other is down. After losing my job, it was my turn to be on the downside for a while. He grew to understand and accept the time and space I needed to make this book a reality. And he let me know when it was time to pay attention to him.

Erna and David Brout, my mother and uncle, read my earliest pages and encouraged me to keep writing. They influenced significant elements and reminded me to always cut words and shorten sentences.

Bonnie Brout, my sister, became my friend. She was there for me in ways we had never figured out to be for each other.

She is not a reader, but she lived through and influenced these pages. Along with Elisha Iozzi, she brought her artistic genius to designing the book cover.

Members of my second family, the Hutchinsons, were always ready to listen when I was ready to talk. I thank Evy, Paul, LouAnn, Phil, Martha, Alan, and Nanc for being there during some of my darkest days.

Pat Beauchamp, Tracy Collie, Rob Fullerton, Ellen Hepp, and Stephanie Kirk were there for me in ways I will always treasure. They listened patiently to endless ups and downs and helped me stay resilient. Patty Delany saw me through my false positive—one of my worst nightmares. Vicki Grey provided support and marketing brilliance right when I needed it.

Dan Soderberg, my early job search whisperer, asked one question that changed how I spent my time. Lynne Williams sparked the creation of my next chapter by asking me to introduce myself at a career transitions meeting. That was the first time I said, "I help people perfect their words." Melanie Lewis, my guardian angel, cultivated the path to my extraordinary job at Gap International.

A mis amigas, Carol Meinhardt y Dana Navaline, muchísimas gracias por siempre escucharme y practicar a español. Carol Baldwin, my hairdresser at Nirvana Hair Gallery, stood by me (literally) as each installment went live. Scott Scioli made this a stronger book to publish. Brent Snyder helped me establish and keep my technology working.

Raia King provided wisdom that guided me from "How will I ever ..." to "I will self-publish, and it will be professional quality." I treasure every word of feedback I received from my first readers: Pat Beauchamp, Erna and David Brout, Andrea Fetterman, Bryan Hutchinson, LouAnn Muir Hutchinson, Stephanie Kirk, Bayne Northern, and Dan Soderberg.

Upon the second anniversary of losing my job, each received a draft manuscript. Turning out to be a much rougher draft than I imagined, it was comforting to learn that famous authors refer affectionately to first drafts as garbage, ugly, and vomit. Please join me in thanking my readers for slogging through the muck and providing notes that made a huge difference to these pages—especially those who had experienced difficult job losses of their own.

My career coach and the president/CEO of the outplacement firm guided me through many essential activities. Vicki Shinoda, LCSW, helped me ride the tidal waves as they became a gentle ocean current while I wrote my next chapter. Paulette Gabriel, my first leadership coach and a special person in my life, graciously offered and wrote the foreword. She always told the truth, and helped me find strengths amid self-criticism and doubt.

Every writer needs a great editor—I had four. Andrea Fetterman helped me refine the overall structure and flow of the book. Anita Smith used her surgical precision to help perfect each sentence. Third was WordRake®, a powerful tool that "rakes" through any Microsoft Word and Outlook copy to identify words that could be cut. Number four was me. Like most writers, I edit my writing incessantly—and it can *always* be improved.

As I learned what it takes to evolve a book from the first draft to publication, I chuckled when family members asked if I was done yet—and didn't quite understand why I wasn't even close. At some point, "It's finished." had to be declared—knowing I would find things to change the moment I saw the book in print.

ABOUT THE AUTHOR

Writing and editing for over 30 years, Nancy Brout collaborates with clients to perfect content they have drafted or envisioned.

With broad business experience and a graduate degree in psychology, she finds great satisfaction in guiding people to discover what they want to do professionally, and then make it happen.

Nancy's proven job search methods come from being a Hard-to-Define Professional who changed careers three times by applying for advertised jobs rather than networking. After 20 years in one company, she conducted four search strategies, discovered work she was meant to do, helped clients gain confidence and find new jobs, and landed in an amazing job of her own. Nancy lives in Pennsylvania and can be reached at: nbrout@WordsPerfected.net.

Made in the USA
Middletown, DE
17 September 2018